REMINISCENCES,

SKETCHES AND ADDRESSES

SELECTED FROM MY PAPERS

DURING A MINISTRY OF FORTY-FIVE YEARS

IN MISSISSIPPI, LOUISIANA AND TEXAS.

BY

REV. J. R. HUTCHISON, D.D.

HOUSTON, TEXAS:
E. H. CUSHING, PUBLISHER.
1874.

Entered according to Act of Congress, in the year 1874, by
E. H. CUSHING,
In the Office of the Librarian of Congress, at Washington.

LANGE, LITTLE & CO.,
PRINTERS, ELECTROTYPERS AND STEREOTYPERS.
108 TO 114 WOOSTER STREET, N. Y.

CONTENTS.

PERSONAL RECOLLECTIONS.

During my long residence in the Southwest, I have often been surprised at the want of interest manifested in the preservation of family reminiscences. Many grandchildren know not where their grandparents came from. An adventurer from the North strays off to this new land of promise, forms new family ties, and finally dies and is buried, and carries to an unmarked grave much which his sons should have been proud to remember and transmit to their posterity. Even titles to land have been forfeited by this neglect of parental or filial obligation. I have almost literally helped in deciphering the dim records of old gravestones to aid Northern claimants to establish heirship to Southern dead men's property. What an unexpected surprise to a descendant of Dr. Timothy Dwight, if in some old Georgia cabin were yet to turn up a quaint tin box, containing the long-lost original title-deeds of his father and General Lyman to all that rich section of country embracing the city of Natchez and the surrounding region! But it is in reference to what is more precious than lost land-titles that I would infuse a new spirit into every rising Southern village. Pride of ancestry is as valuable at the South as at the North, and should contribute as much in building up a Texan family as a New England town.

I was born in Columbia County, in the State of Pennsylvania, on the 12th of February, 1807. I am a lineal descendant, by my father's side, of those noble patriots who maintained the celebrated siege of Derry, in the north of Ireland, against the combined forces of James of England and the king of France. This siege lasted from December, 1688, to August, 1689. From this dates the "Protestant succession," and William, Prince of Orange, ascended the British throne. The sufferings of the people, during that memorable occasion, equal anything to be found in the records of English history. For several generations after coming to this country, there was preserved in my family a *knife* with which the original owner, of the name of Hutchison, dug up roots beneath the walls of Derry upon which to subsist during the horrors of that terrible siege. (Read Macaulay's England and Charlotte Elizabeth's Sketches.)

At what time my family crossed the Atlantic I am unable to say. I think it was in 1732. But my grandfather, Joseph Hutchison, was a native American, and was born in Dauphin County, Pennsylvania, near the spot where now stands the city of Harrisburg, the capital of the State.

In early times the Susquehanna, as well as all other Northern rivers, abounded in shad. It was customary, immediately after wheat-harvest, in those days, for neighbors to assemble together, and in a short time, by dragging the seine, to supply their families with fish sufficient to last during the ensuing winter. During my grandfather's boyhood, in one of those assemblies of the farmers for fishing, a violent thunderstorm coming up, my great-grandfather took shelter under a tree on a small island opposite where the city of Harrisburg now stands, and was instantly killed by a stroke of lightning.

Soon after the birth of my father, my grandfather and his brother Samuel removed to that part of Northumberland County (Pennsylvania) now called Columbia

County, where they purchased a large tract of land on the Chillisquaque Creek, near the present village of Washingtonville, and midway between Danville and Milton. This purchase included Bosley's Mills, where there was a small fort during the Revolutionary War. This neighborhood was the scene of many stirring incidents in the early settlement of the country. I remember, when a child, of hearing many romantic and thrilling incidents of border warfare and Indian barbarities. Whole settlements were often broken up, and the inhabitants killed or scattered. It was customary for families, on a sudden incursion of Indians, to hide their most valuable articles of property and flee to some more populous and better defended locality. I have, when a child, seen various articles, such as pots, gridirons, garments, etc., turned up by the plough in my grandfather's field, where they were buried in haste by the fleeing inhabitants. The place of my nativity is about thirty miles south of the valley of Wyoming, the scene of a massacre by Indians and Tories which will be forever remembered in the annals of the country.

I will here relate an incident which I heard from my mother, and which illustrates the state of the times and the character of the people. At the massacre of Wyoming the whole region was aroused and the people fled to the block-houses. My mother, then a small girl, and residing with an aunt, had to flee with the rest. Hungry and exhausted, and gaining a respite from their savage pursuers, she and her young friends supplied themselves with a quantity of red apples, taken from a crib on the wayside which had been abandoned by its owners. When this act of taking the fruit came to the knowledge of the parents and guardians of the children, it was construed into a species of theft, and though in the direction of their Indian pursuers, all were required to retrace their steps and replace the apples, and thus run the risk of meeting the Indians. Such a requirement in a parent or guardian in our day would have been viewed by most persons as a cruel exposure of the life of a child. But in those days children were taught elevated views of morality, and the slightest approach to theft or falsehood was most promptly punished. The effect upon the mind of my mother of this severe test of her courage and obedience was most beneficial, and she often alluded to the incident in her family as exerting a happy influence on her character in all subsequent life.

My father, Andrew Hutchison, the second son of my grandfather, was a man of fine personal appearance, of medium size, of great muscular activity, and was very popular in his neighborhood. Possessing a better education than most other young men of his day, his services were in great demand as a surveyor, a writer of deeds, letters, etc. His earlier days were spent in attending the mills of his father and uncle, and towards manhood he was engaged in teaching school. He married young and settled on a small farm adjoining that of my grandfather. In 1813 he was chosen colonel of a regiment of militia which was ordered to the northern frontier to engage in the war with Great Britain. Though but six years old at the time, I remember every important event that occurred—the frequent mustering of the militia, my father's gay military dress, the patriotic songs, and many other thrilling incidents of a time of war. At last, my father's departure for Black Rock, my mother's tears, and the adieus of friends are all remembered. Equally well do I remember my father's return in a short time—his illness, his death, in dead of winter, amid the deep snow, the grave (the first I had ever seen), and the painful impression I long entertained of his confinement in the cold ground. The first dead man I ever saw was my father.

After my father's death my mother continued to reside on the same farm, and support and educate her family of five children, the eldest of whom was ten years old. She was a woman of remarkable energy of character. At this distant day, her many virtues, rendered prominent by her heroic struggles with comparative poverty, stand out before my mind in bold relief. She was a woman of great decision of character, and in great demand as a counselor in the neighborhood. After my father's death (who was a professor of religion and maintained family worship) my mother continued the practice of praying in her family, and maintained it while she lived. She labored faithfully, and often with tears, to impress upon the minds of her children the importance of youthful piety. My earliest and most important religious impressions were produced by her instructions and prayers. She was firm but tender in domestic discipline, often weeping when using the rod, mingling tears with correction. Precious is the memory of my mother.

In recalling the scenes and incidents of my childhood, I wish here to record my unbounded admiration of the character of the Scotch-Irish Presbyterians, who were the principal settlers of the middle counties of Pennsylvania, and of many other States of the Union. Much has been said, and with justice, of the noble characte. of the Puritans, the Huguenots, and cavaliers. But the influence which has been exerted upon the nation by the Scotch-Irish element, spread out as it now is throughout Pennsylvania, Western Virginia, the Carolinas, New York, Eastern Mississippi, and all the Western States, can never be fully appreciated. I glory in my descent from such a noble stock. My impression also is that much more information was communicated, when I was young, by *oral* instruction, than at the present time. Old people rehearsed by the fireside the incidents of their early days and what they had heard from their fathers, and the young were eager listeners. Though books and newspapers and traveling afford greater means of imparting knowledge now than then, yet I doubt whether youth are better taught in useful things, or have the more important faculties both of mind and heart better developed at the present day than formerly.

My mother died when I was eight years old.

> "My mother, when I learned that thou wast dead,
> Say, wast thou conscious of the tears I shed?
> Hover'd thy spirit o'er thy sorrowing son,
> Wretch, even then, life's journey just begun?"

Immediately after the death of my mother, our family (five in number) were scattered among our relatives. I became a member of the family of my uncle, the Rev. John Hutchison, of Mifflintown, Juniata County (Pennsylvania). He was the only full brother of my father, by whom I was adopted and educated. He was a superior man in almost every respect. He graduated at Dickinson College (Pennsylvania), under the presidency of the celebrated Dr. Nesbitt. In 1805 he assumed the pastoral charge of the churches of Mifflintown and Lost Creek, where he continued to labor until his death, which took place on the 11th of November, 1844, having retained the charge of the same churches for thirty-nine years. Few ministers of the Gospel in Central Pennsylvania have lived more honored and died more lamented than he. He was a man of great purity and simplicity—an entertaining companion, a firm friend, a wise counselor, a patient endurer of reproach, and a fearless defender of the faith. He seemed to have possessed an intuitive knowledge of human nature. The motives of men seemed to reveal themselves at once to his view. He was the last man on whom any one could palm an imposition. He was also famed throughout the country for great neatness and system in all the ordinary affairs of life. His house, his apparel, his domestic economy, his traveling equipage, were all expressive of the order and native sense of propriety which characterized him. His attainments as a scholar and theologian were of a highly respectable order, and for many years he was a prominent member of Huntington Presbytery. Like many of the Presbyterian clergymen of the Northern States, he devoted much of his time and attention to classical studies. His academy was known for more than thirty years as the best in all Central Pennsylvania, and his Latin and Greek scholars always took a high position upon entering any of the colleges of the State. A large number of the professional men in the middle counties of Pennsylvania were trained under his tuition. At the age of thirteen I commenced the study of the Latin and Greek languages. When I arrived at the age of seventeen I became his assistant, and thus secured the means of finishing my college course. I thus had an opportunity of attaining a degree of accuracy in classical studies which has proved of essential advantage to me in all my subsequent life.

I would here remark that, after having been for a long time professor of the Latin, Greek, and Hebrew languages, it is my opinion that better classical scholars were made fifty years ago than now. Several causes may be assigned for the present degeneracy: *First.* In the present day boys are taught *too many things* in connection with languages. *Second.* The many new grammars and new editions of the classics, with their various helps, explanations, and English notes, are no real improvement on the old ones. These modern *helps* to study *prevent* study. *Third.* Teachers have degenerated. Now, our teachers are young men, nice young men, possessed of great self-esteem, intending to study law or medicine, and making teaching only a stepping-stone to something else. In my early day, teachers were usually Presbyterian ministers, or candidates for the ministry, who loved to teach, who knew how to teach, and who had a reputation to sustain. *Fourth.* Boys in the present day are more difficult to be taught than formerly. They are not taught as much at home as in former years. Especially, their memories are not drilled, as they once were, by committing to memory the General Assembly's shorter catechism. Consequently, they are not so capable of committing with accuracy the Latin and Greek grammars. I have always noticed that the sons of old-fashioned Presbyterians usually make the best classical scholars. Their superior religious training renders them more susceptible of a thorough classical training. From these and other considerations, I am more and more convinced that if we would have better scholarship in our colleges, we must have our youth prepared, not in preparatory schools, but by the pastors of our churches, or in parochial schools under their care.

I resided in Mifflintown from 1815 to 1824. Those years constitute the most important period of my life. I can now trace back almost all my habits and my peculiarities of character to that period. My residence in my uncle's family imposed upon me the duty of work as well as of study. Gardening, the providing of fire-wood in winter, the care of horses, cows, etc., were, fortunately for me, combined with intellectual culture, thus giving the best means of developing the powers both of mind and body. Having also access to all kinds of books, I then formed habits of general reading, and by some assistance and close application I qualified myself for entering the Junior Class in Jefferson College. How often do I now revert in thought to those pleasant by-gone days. Within a few months past, I was once more permitted to revisit those scenes of my youth, after an absence of twenty years. But alas, how changed! Nature was there. There were the bold Alleghany Mountains, the green hills, the beautiful stream of the Juniata. But almost all the companions of my youth and my kindred were no more. Strange faces looked upon me, and I found myself more at home among the tombs of the dead than in the dwellings of the living.

In the Spring of 1825, I left Mifflintown for Jefferson College, Cannonsburg (Pennsylvania). Stopping at Pittsburg for a few days, I had the opportunity of seeing the distinguished General La Fayette, the companion of Washington, the early and devoted friend of the struggling American colonies, who was then revisiting the scenes of his early battles in the cause of liberty, and whose progress through the country resembled a continued Roman triumph.

I entered the Junior Class in Jefferson College half advanced. The class consisted of thirty members. Jefferson College, at the time I entered it, was in its zenith. It was the most prominent institution west of the Alleghany Mountains, and under the long presidency of Dr. Matthew Brown, it furnished the ministry which gave character to the Presbyterian Church in all that vast region of country. Rev. Aaron Williams and Rev. Dr. A. T. McGill, now professor at Princeton (New Jersey) were my associates in study. I entered the Theological Seminary at Princeton in the Fall of 1826.

My health failing in two years, I became an inmate for a few months in the family of the Rev. Dr. E. S. Ely, pastor of the Pine Street Church, Philadelphia. Dr. Ely was at that time at the height of his fame as a popular preacher, a leader in ecclesiastical courts, a man of wealth, a skillful financier, a patron of all public institutions, and the liberal friend and helper of all young men seeking the ministry of the Gospel. Though a man of eccentricity, "full of fat, fun, and fortune," yet he exerted for many years a controlling influence in all matters connected with the Presbyterian Church in the Middle States. About the year 1831, he became a prominent leader in an effort to found a great Western city on the Mississippi River. Many persons, by his influence and wealth, were induced to unite with him in this plausible scheme. Many widows, and others having the control of small means throughout the country, cast in their lot with him and invested their all—and Marion City, near Hannibal, for a short time bid fair to rise to some eminence. But the pecuniary revulsion which spread over the whole country in 1837–8, fell upon all such enterprises with a stunning blow. The greater portion of the people assembled at Marion City were dispersed, their means were squandered, their health and spirits broken, their chief leaders abandoned the project, and Dr. Ely, broken in fortune and spirits, returned to Philadelphia. Though Dr. Ely's course in the incidents just narrated, and also in the part he took in the division of the Presbyterian Church into Old and New School, is certainly to be condemned, yet he deserved great honor while he lived, and his memory should be still cherished since his death, for the great good he accomplished in the earlier period of his life. Multitudes of young men were aided by him in their efforts to enter the ministry. His residence in Philadelphia was the abode of elegant hospitality. The Jefferson Medical College was founded mainly by his efforts. Many widows and orphans were clothed and fed by his money; and for many years he expended the whole of his salary from his congregation in acts of benevolence. I must place on record this tribute to the name of Dr. Ezra Stiles Ely.

On the 22d of April, 1829, and when in my twenty-second year, I was licensed to preach the Gospel by the Presbytery of Philadelphia, at Frankfort, a village some miles from the city. Two other young men were licensed at the same time: Rev. Nicholas Murray, now deceased, for many years pastor of the First Presbyterian Church at Elizabethtown (New Jersey), a man eminent for his learning, and particularly a popular writer against Catholicism, over the name of "Kirwan." The other was the Rev. Alexander Aikman, of Bordentown (New Jersey), a young man of varied attainments in learning and theology, who was sent to New Orleans in 1832 to take charge of the First Presbyterian Church in that city, rendered vacant by the deposition from the ministry of Rev. Theodore Clapp by the Presbytery of Mississippi. Mr. Aikman commenced his labors under most encouraging auspices, and did much to divest Presbyterianism of the odium under which it had been suffering for many years from the misrepresentations of Mr. Clapp. But in a short time his health failed, and, leaving New Orleans, he came to Natchez, where, after lingering for some weeks, he died. His sun went down at noon.

My first appearance in the pulpit was at Norristown, in Montgomery County, about twenty miles from Philadelphia. In the month of October, 1829, I started for Mississippi, landed at Rodney, walked out to the residence of Dr. Rush Nutt (two miles from the river);

remained in that vicinity, preaching at Rodney and Bethel, until July following, when I removed to Baton Rouge (Louisiana); succeeded Rev. John Dorrance as pastor of the church; married on the 20th of September, 1832; in January, 1834, became connected with the College of Louisiana at Jackson; went as a delegate to the General Assembly at Pittsburg in May, 1836; visited New England during the summer of that year; returned to Louisiana in the fall; accepted a call to the church of Vicksburg, with a salary of $3,000, where I remained pastor for six years; then accepted a professorship in Oakland College, which I held for twelve years; then resigned in 1854, and removed to Covington (Louisiana), where I had charge of a private seminary of learning for three years, preaching also during the same time at Covington and Madisonville; then removed to New Orleans, and purchased the property called the Brick House Station, on the Carrollton Railroad, where I established a male high school, and, at the same time, preaching at Carrollton Church and the Prytania Street Church in the city. In the fall of 1860 I removed to Houston, in Texas, and took charge of the Public Academy; was removed from the institution by the military authorities of the Confederate States, which converted the establishment into a hospital; then opened a private male and female academy at Turner's Hall, where I also preached to the Presbyterian Church until their edifice, which was burned down, was rebuilt. At the close of my superintendence of the Public Academy of Houston I had one hundred and fifty male and female pupils.

At the close of the war, in 1865, I became deeply concerned as to my duty in reference to the spiritual desolations of the villages and churches within the bounds of the Brazos Presbytery, and accessible by railroads from the city of Houston. My convictions of duty in this matter led me to open a correspondence with my ministerial brethren in the region referred to, asking their advice and co-operation, and inquiring whether my entrance into the field would meet their approval, and in no way interfere with their respective fields of labor. From all with whom I corresponded I received cordial encouragement. And then the question presented itself to my mind, "How shall I obtain a pecuniary support?" for, up to the close of the war, no reorganization of the Presbyterian Church had been effected within the bounds of the Confederate States. The Corresponding Secretary of the Board of Domestic Missions at Philadelphia, intimated, through a third party, that, on evidence of "loyalty," a sufficient salary would be secured to me, if I would enter upon the same field. Such a proposition I could not entertain. In the fall of 1866, in a conference with some prominent members of the Church, I was urged to carry out my original purpose; and the late Thomas M. Bagby, of Houston, and Mr. James Sorley, of Galveston, placed in my hands $50 each, as a salary for the month of January, in 1867, to justify me to leave my home and commence my work. It was agreed and understood that I should explore the whole field, ascertain the Presbyterian element in each destitute community, preach the Gospel, organize churches, and prepare the way for the settlement of pastors and stated supplies. On the 1st of January, 1867, I commenced my labors, visiting as soon as possible the towns of Hempstead, Chappell Hill, Navesota, Richmond, Harrisburg, Columbus, Alleytown and Beaumont. Within six months from the commencement of the year, I had reorganized the churches of Hempstead and Chappell Hill, and organized new churches at Navesota and Bryan City. During the first year of my mission, I received no formal recognition from the Presbytery, and no pecuniary aid, excepting from the two brethren above named, and from the voluntary contributions of the people to whom I ministered. And during no single month, from the commencement of my services until now (1874), has my entire income ever exceeded one hundred dollars. At all the points where I have labored, I have always been emphatic, both in my private and public announcements, that so soon as any congregation may think itself able to call a pastor or stated supply of its own, I should at once retire from the field. The people of Navesota and Bryan City can testify to the truth of my present assertion.

In recapitulating my ministerial life of forty-five years, I wish here devoutly to record the goodness of a special Providence in prolonging my days to the commencement of my sixty-seventh year, preserving me amid sickness, amid epidemics, amid war, blessing me with a faithful and loving wife, and ten grown and affectionate children. Though I have had the yellow fever more than once, yet I have never been seriously interrupted in my profession by any dangerous or protracted sickness. I have never lost the confidence and esteem of any community in which I have lived. I served the church of Baton Rouge for three years; the College of Louisiana, three years; the Vicksburg Church, six years; Oakland College, twelve years; Covington, three years; New Orleans, three years; and Houston, fifteen years. I have married three hundred couples, and received in marriage fees four thousand three hundred dollars.

PRESBYTERIANISM IN THE SOUTHWEST.

ORIGIN OF OAKLAND COLLEGE—MURDER OF PRESIDENT CHAMBERLAIN.

OAKLAND COLLEGE is located in Claiborne County (Mississippi), thirty-five miles north of the city of Natchez, and five miles east of the Mississippi River. Rodney is the nearest landing. Bruinsburg, three miles north, is the spot where General Grant crossed the river and gained possession of the rear of the city of Vicksburg, and soon that city fell. Oakland is situated in a region of country rendered interesting from many reminiscences of early times. Here was the scene of some characteristic incidents in the life of General Andrew Jackson. A few miles from the college was the residence of Blennerhassett. Here was the place of the capture of Aaron Burr. In this vicinity was the plantation of the amiable, patriotic, and lamented General Zachary Taylor. This region also derives much interest from the visits and labors of some of the earliest pioneers of Presbyterianism in the Southwest. Rickhow, and Smylie, and Montgomery—the last lately gone to his reward after a long life of labor in the Master's vineyard, the two former still living at an advanced age—here came, when the dew of their youth was upon them, and laid the foundation of our churches. Here visited and preached Schermerhorn, and S. J. Mills, and Larned, and Bullen, and many others whose praise is in our Southern Zion. The eccentric Lorenzo Dow here rode his mule and blew his horn, and attracted crowds of the first settlers, preaching on housetops and haystacks, resembling Peter the Hermit, who once marshalled all Europe under the Crusader's banner.

The origin of Oakland College may be traced to a meeting of Presbyterian ministers, held in the town of Baton Rouge, Louisiana, in April, 1829. Some circumstances had occurred previous to this meeting which had particularly attracted the attention of Presbyterians to the subject of Southern education. There was not, at that time, a single college, prepared to give a regular collegiate education, within the States of Louisiana, Mississippi, and the territory of Arkansas—containing a population at that time of more than three hundred thousand souls, and a tract of country of more than one hundred and forty-five thousand square miles, embracing the growing city of New Orleans and other cities—with a soil capable of sustaining a vast population. Efforts had been made by the Legislature of Louisiana, with princely liberality, to establish several institutions of learning, all of which had virtually failed. In the State of Mississippi exertions had been made for nearly thirty years, and large donations from the general government, and from corporations and individuals, had been expended; and yet not one individual was known to have been graduated. The religious community had done nothing.

After viewing these facts, and having a full interchange of sentiments, the clergymen above referred to concluded that they would fail in their duty, and forfeit the character of their Church, as the great champion of learning, if they did not make an effort to meet the claims of the country, and provide means for a thorough Southern education. A committee was accordingly appointed who, after an extensive correspondence, continued through several months, called a meeting of the friends of education at Bethel Church, two miles from the present location of the college, on the 14th of January, 1830. This meeting was composed of gentlemen from the parishes of East Baton Rouge, East Feliciana, and West Feliciana, Louisiana; and from the counties of Claiborne, Amite, Wilkinson, Adams, Jefferson, Warren, Hinds, and Madison, in Mississippi, and continued six days. The following resolution was presented:

Resolved, That it is expedient to establish and endow an institution of learning within our bounds, which, when complete, shall embrace the usual branches of science and literature taught in the colleges of our country, together with a preparatory English and Grammar School, and Theological Professorship, or Seminary.

This resolution was sustained by gentlemen from every part of the country represented in the meeting; and after considering it for three days, it was unanimously adopted. A subscription was immediately opened to supply the requisite funds. Twelve thousand dollars were contributed for the purchase of a site and the erection of necessary buildings. Committees were appointed to prepare a constitution, to view the various locations which had been spoken of, and to make all necessary arrangements for opening the school.

The Presbytery of Mississippi, embracing, at that time, all the Presbyterian ministers in Louisiana, Mississippi, and Arkansas, received the proposed seminary under its care, adopted a constitution, appointed a Board of Trustees and the President of the college, and fixed the location within three miles of Bethel Church, in Claiborne County, Mississippi. On the 14th of May the school opened with three pupils, who had accompanied the President, the Rev. Jeremiah Chamberlain, D.D., from Jackson, Louisiana, where he had been presiding for some time over the "College of Louisiana."

On the 2d of July, 1830, the first clearing was begun on the magnificent Oak Ridge, now occupied by the college buildings. At the end of the session, March 28th, the school consisted of sixty-five pupils. The two more advanced formed a sophomore class, and there were five in the freshman class; the remainder were in the English and classical schools. The President instructed the two college classes and the classical school in the languages; and his brother, Mr. John Chamberlain, afterwards professor of chemistry and natural philosophy, instructed the classes in mathematics and in the English school. In the winter of 1831, a charter was received from the legislature of the State. In 1833, the first commencement was held; and Mr. James M. Smylie, recent Vice-Chancellor of the State of Mississippi, was the first graduate of Oakland College. His classmate, William Montgomery, son of Rev. William Montgomery, one of our oldest ministers, who expected to receive his degree at the same time, was removed by death about three weeks before the commencement. This is believed to be the first commencement *south of Tennessee*, and Judge Smylie is the first native Mississippian who received the degree of A. B. in his own State.

Such was the origin of Oakland College, an institution which has aided in the education of nearly one thousand native youth, and which now has on the roll of its graduates one hundred and twenty alumni, who are scattered throughout the Southwest, and occupied in the cultivation of the soil or in the learned professions. And the writer believes that there is not on the list of the graduates of Oakland College a single name upon which rests a blemish of dishonor or immorality. And the large number of those educated young men who assemble annually in the groves and halls of their alma mater, is a pleasing token of their interest and affection, and a guarantee of what the institution may hereafter expect from the influence and character of her own sons.

The necessary buildings and accommodations for students and teachers have been provided as the wants of the institution have required. There are, at this time, about thirty cottages for the occupancy of the pupils; residences for the President and professors; two handsome halls for the literary societies, with libraries attached; a college library of upwards of four thousand volumes; a philosophical, chemical, and astronomical apparatus, which cost nearly $4,000; a main college of brick, one hundred and twelve by sixty, containing a college chapel, prayer hall, lecture rooms, and other requisite accommodations. The institution has never received any aid from the State or general government. Its funds have been provided entirely from private liberality. And these funds would now be sufficient to sustain the college, were it not for some unfortunate investments a few years since in the banks of the State.

We shall conclude this brief history of Oakland College, by stating a recent occurrence, which, at the time, cast a deep gloom over the institution, and filled the whole land with astonishment and grief. The President and professors had been performing their quiet and laborious duties, unconscious of being the objects of any great amount of popular dislike or favor, when, during the pendency of the election in the State of Mississippi, in the summer of 1851, for members to the State Convention, the faculty were accused by individuals, and by some of the State Rights papers, of giving in their teachings undue favor to the sentiments of the Union Party. These clamors gained ground, until, during the election in September, handbills were circulated directly charging the faculty with highly improper conduct in this respect. These charges were mildly but firmly repelled in a card signed by the President of the college. The leaders of the two parties were General H. S. Foot and Jefferson Davis. A citizen of the neighborhood, who had no connection with the college, either as a student or in any other respect, but who deemed himself either personally or politically implicated in the denial of the President, stopped at Dr. Chamberlain's house, on the evening of the 5th of September (at a time when the professors and students were absent enjoying the vacation), and called the doctor to his gate. Retaining his seat in his vehicle, he commenced denouncing the doctor in very abusive terms, and made some charge against him, the nature of which was not distinctly heard. Dr. Chamberlain, quietly leaning upon the top rail of his gate on the inside, denied the charge, and said that it could not be proved. Instantly the assailant sprang from his carriage, and knocked the doctor down with the butt-end of a loaded whip. As the doctor rose, or attempted to rise, he was knocked down again; and as he attempted to rise the second time, he was stabbed to the heart with a bowie-knife. All this took place in the presence of the female members of the family, whose screams were heard at a distance, and brought the doctor's son-in-law to the spot. He found the doctor standing up, but bleeding, and the murderer, outside of the gate, wiping his bloody knife upon his handkerchief. The doctor had strength to walk to the house, but, on reaching the middle of the open passage, he exclaimed, "I am killed;" and, sinking on the floor, he immediately expired.

Thus fell a great and good man. Conciliatory in all his intercourse, bland and courteous in his manners, even when smarting under unmerited obloquy, but brave and firm as a martyr for principle, and ready to stand in his lot for the cause of truth and right, at all times and against any odds, he at last fell to appease the bitterness of partisan malice and personal hate. For more than a quarter of a century he devoted himself, with a zeal, a self-abnegation, and a success unparalleled, to the cause of Southern education. Mainly by his efforts and sacrifices, a college has been founded in Mississippi which has educated and graduated more young men than all other colleges south of Tennessee. And after all the labors, the trials, and the temptations of his long career, he has left the memory of no one act which his bitterest enemy will now venture to censure.

We would here simply remark that a coroner's jury, consisting of fourteen citizens, pronounced the act by which Dr. Chamberlain came to his death, *murder*. The perpetrator of the crime, on the second day after the deed, committed suicide, and passed beyond the reach of all human tribunals.

Although President Chamberlain thus fell, so cruelly, so suddenly, yet Oakland College did not fall with him. It still lives, and shall live, a monument of his fame, and a blessing to the present and future generations. And as it is the ordainment of heaven that martyr blood becomes precious seed, whence springs undying truth, we doubt not that the great principle, in this instance as in others, will be fully developed. No sooner was Oakland's chief founder and first President cut down, than the true and firm friends of the institution began to rally. Precisely one year has elapsed since the sad event occurred; and in that year much has been done to place the college upon a firm and permanent basis. Upwards of $60,000 have been contributed to pay its debts, and meet its more immediate wants. The name of its first President is to be perpetuated, by the investment of a permanent fund, to be called the "Chamberlain Fund," the interest of which is to pay the salary of his successor. Overtures have been made from a distant source to found a professorship of Natural Science; and from various other sources are cheering indications that this infant seat of learning, which has struggled so long and done so much, will yet become the glory of the South, and a rich blessing to the future generations.

The present faculty are: Rev. R. L. Stanton, D.D., President, and Professor of Moral Sciences; Rev. J. R. Hutchison, D.D., Professor of Latin, Greek, and Hebrew Languages; T. Newton Wilson, A.M., Professor of Mathematics; W. Le Roy Brown, A.M., Professor of Chemistry and Natural Philosophy; H. B. Underhill, A.M., Principal of the Preparatory Department; James Collier, Esq., Steward.

September 6, 1852.

HISTORY

OF THE

CHURCH OF BETHEL AND RODNEY,

(NEAR OAKLAND COLLEGE, MISS.).

IN the year 1828 the Legislature of Mississippi granted a charter to that portion of Bethel Congregation now worshiping in Rodney, under the name of the "Presbyterian Congregation of Petit Gulf," and designated David Hunt, John H. Savage, John Watt, and James Couden as trustees, with the power of appointing their successors. At the same time and in the same act, the Legislature granted a charter to that portion of the congregation worshiping at Bethel, two miles from the college, under the style and name of the "Presbyterian Congregation of Bethel," and named William Young, Lewellin Price, John Magruder, and Smith C. Daniel trustees of the same, with similar power of electing their successors. The first building for public worship erected by this double congregation was located in the rear of the plantations of the late Smith Hubbard and James M. Batchelor, about three miles east of the town of Rodney. The prominent actors in this new enterprise were Daniel Hunt, John Bolls, Smith Hubbard, Dr. Rush Nutt, John Murdock, Sen., M. McClutchy, and also Matthew Bolls. The last named was the son of John Bolls, who was a man distinguished in the early annals of the church in this region, and whose name appears on several church books—a man who, though little in stature, was mighty in faith, swift of foot, great at a bear-hunt or in taming wild steers, the first to hear of a new preacher coming to the settlement and ride thirty miles to see him; mighty in cutting down trees to build meeting-houses, and who had the honor of being imprisoned in the calaboose in Natchez for being a heretic, having been betrayed to the priest by a stranger whom he had sheltered and nursed in sickness. His son Matthew was as large again as his father, tall and gaunt, a wit and a poet, whose quaint sayings, famous "book of chronicles," and imitations of Burns' poems convulsed many a circle with laughter. Forty years ago, he had much to say about early times —how he soon outgrew his father, but still dared not disobey him—how he never regularly wore shoes and stockings until after he was married—how, for the want of saddles and bridles, he and his companions would seize wild horses, noose them with grape-vines, and ride furiously to merry-makings. He knew something by experience of the toilsome mode of removing cotton from the cotton-seed, before the introduction of the cotton-gin. Then every little boy and girl, white and black, had to bend themselves to the task, just as in picking wool; and when a sufficient amount was prepared, a large barrel, like an empty tobacco hogshead, was filled, shafts were attached to each end, and it was trundled across hills and cane-brakes to Selsertown, to be pressed into bags. Cotton was precious in those days, bringing forty cents per pound. Matthew Boll's account of the first meeting to build the church building, of which we are speaking, was characteristic of the men and the times. One thought that it would come to nothing. Another, that it would break up the races down at Greenville and spoil their Sunday sports. Another, that it might help to keep the women and children in order. But all concluded to try it, and each put down a dollar to begin with. Noble effort! In that little gathering were men who learned from that time to give their thousands to the cause of Christ and education. In a short time, "the little church down Hubbard's lane—the little church round the corner"—became inconvenient; and about 1824 efforts were made to build two houses, one at Bethel cross-roads, two miles from Oakland College, and another at Rodney.

The first stated minister of the church was Rev. Samuel Hunter, a native of Ireland, who preached at different points in the vicinity; and about 1826 organized "Bethel Church," an offshoot of the Old Bethel, near Fayette, made up of members principally from the old "Bayou Pierre Church," which worshiped formerly in a log building on the road now leading from Mrs. Crane's residence to Port Gibson, and near the residence of Mr. Venable. The place where the house stood can only now be identified by a few old trees and sunken graves. I know the spot. As early as 1824, the old Presbytery of Mississippi met in session there. There were Rickhow, and Montgomery, and Patterson, and Chase, and others. A young man from New England offered himself as a candidate for the ministry, was licensed (the first licensure ever witnessed by the people), and after laboring a short time at St. Francisville and Baton Rouge, returned to his home, and within two years past has ceased from his labors. He was the Rev. Thomas Savage, late of Londonderry Presbytery. A later incident connected with this lonely spot is familiar from personal presence. Nearly twenty years ago, two horsemen, on a sultry day, turned aside at these old graves to repose beneath the shade, and have time to get to Oakland at sundown. Plucking some wild grapes from overhead, they stretched themselves on the grass to rest and talk. Being both given to being merry and sad as occasion offered, the time and the place gave food to both extremes of temperament. They talked about the past, the present, and the future. They then arose and departed. One remains until this day to record the past. The other (three days after) fell by the hand of an assassin! (See History of Oakland College.)

The original members composing the "Bayou Pierre Church," and then incorporated into Bethel Church, were John Bolls, elder (noble old man, with a little body but a big soul, and who *loaned* himself about among the churches as an elder until other elders arose), Mrs. Catherine Crane, Lewellin Price (grandfather of Rev. Robert Price), William Young, Clara Young, Dr. Rush Nutt, Mrs. Nutt, Mrs. Elisa Kerr, David Hunt, Mrs. Ann F. Hunt, and others. Early in the spring of 1828, Mr. Hunter retired from the care of Bethel and Rodney churches, and the Rev. Zebulon Butler took charge of the congregation in conjunction with the church of Port Gibson, for one year. In November, the Rev. J. R. Hutchison came from Princeton Theological Seminary, and preached at Rodney as stated supply until the following July, when he removed to Baton Rouge and succeeded Rev. John Dorrance, who returned to Pennsylvania. While J. R. Hutchison preached at Rodney, there were but two members of the Presbyterian Church residing in the place, although the village contained a larger population than at present. Yet almost all the heads of families in the town formed themselves into a Bible Class and were instructed weekly in the Holy Scriptures. The first place used for public worship was the bar-room of a house of entertainment. On Sabbath morning the landlord would ring the dinner-bell, wipe the stains of decanters and bottles from the table, bring out an old Bible, and the people would come in. Some objected to the preacher because he was too young; but Matthew Bolls, the great oracle, thought that "if they would give the young man a little time, he would get over that defect." The young man has long since got over that fault. The writer has now lost his raven locks, has put on gray hairs, and is old enough.

Early in 1829 steps were taken to erect the present brick church at Rodney. It was dedicated to the worship of God on the first day of January, 1832, by the preaching of a sermon by Rev. Dr. Chamberlain from Exodus xx. 24: "In all places where I record my name, I will come unto thee and I will bless thee." After the house was finished, it appeared that the builder still held a claim against it of $1,500—which debt was quietly paid by Mr. David Hunt, a princely man, and the building released from all embarrassments.

Early in the spring of 1830 a new element of life and vigor was introduced into this church, by the location of Oakland College within its bounds, towards which the members of the congregation subscribed $12,000. Afterwards the same individuals multiplied their donations to the amount of tens of thousands. The reason why the college was located in so retired a spot, was this: *at that time no town or city in the South-west was deemed sufficiently healthy or sufficiently moral to be the seat of a college.* In addition to his position as president, Dr. Chamberlain preached at Rodney and Bethel alternately for seven years. During that time, in addition to the support of their preacher, the people contributed to the different boards of the church about $1,000 annually. On the 11th of November, 1837, the Rev. J. T. Russell was installed pastor, and resigned in 1842. For the twelve next succeeding years, Rev. J. R. Hutchison, having removed from Vicksburg, acted in the capacity of both professor of ancient languages and pastor of the church. During those years the congregation in its spiritual aspects assumed many interesting features. In 1837, about twenty were added to the church, principally young men connected with the college. In 1845, about fifty persons were added to the communion. During the long term of thirty years, the congregation contributed largely to the boards of the church—to the Tract cause, the Bible Society, Sunday-school Union. The American Colonization Society always was a favorite, and sometimes received from individuals contributions amounting to thousands of dollars. For many years, a few noble planters supported a minister to labor exclusively among their slaves. At one time, forty negroes, valued at $330,000, were liberated and sent to Liberia. An individual (Thomas Freeland) contributed, from 1833 to 1843, $333 annually, to support a missionary in China. The students in the college gave about $300 for the boards of the church. Besides, the Theological Seminary at Maryville (Tennessee), the Natchez Orphan Asylum, etc., received large contributions. O! those were palmy days, gone, never to return.

HOUSTON, TEXAS, *August* 28, 1871.

PHYSICAL SCIENCE.

An Address delivered at Oakland College, on the occasion of the Inauguration of Dr. J. H. Savage, as Professor of Chemistry, August, 1842.

Gentlemen of the Board of Trustees and Faculty:

ALL attentive students of history have remarked that great men and great events have generally appeared in clusters. When one individual of vast enterprise or learning has attracted the gaze and admiration of the world, others, remarkable for similar qualities, have arisen almost simultaneously with him. When great inventions and discoveries have dawned upon the earth, others of a kindred character have sprung up around them.

What is the philosophy of this historic truth?

How do we account for it? By the following simple process:—That waking up and inquisitiveness of the human intellect, which results in the discovery of some new principle, or the development of some new and startling invention, impel it forward in a new career, —a career of universal investigation; and speedily other discoveries and inventions open before it, and reward its newly-awakened energies. In addition to this, all truth is intimately affiliated and interwoven, and any change in one of her departments, speedily extends its influence to every other, and, ere long, *all things become new.* But the chief cause why great events and discoveries have so often appeared simultaneously has been, that without such simultaneous appearance they would have been of no great benefit to the world. Providence seems sometimes designedly to have *held back* the mind of man from the perception of certain great principles because *the world was not ready for them; their time had not yet come.* What worthy advantage could have resulted from the discovery of the *art of printing,* had not mankind about the same time begun to call in question the old and time-hallowed dogma that none but kings and priests should possess power and learning—that it was a sin against God for the common people to investigate political and theological opinions. Hence, the discoveries of Johannes Faust and Martin Luther appeared in close proximity —the one standing ready to aid the other—the power of the *Press* to advance and perpetuate the power of the unshackled *mind.*

This simultaneous appearance of great events and their adaptation the one to the other, was most strikingly displayed in the discovery of America, and those other astonishing discoveries and inventions which appeared at the same time.

About the middle of the fifteenth century, that deep night of intellectual and moral darkness which had brooded over the earth for a thousand years began to break away, and the day began to dawn. Suddenly, as by a common impulse, Europe became the theater of great and marvelous events:—the invention of the mariner's compass—the use of gunpowder—the art of printing—the commencement of the glorious reformation,—and the discovery of a new continent beyond the vast Atlantic! These and a thousand other magnificent discoveries thronged upon each other with pressing haste; when with a steady and triumphant step the peerless form of human intellect arose erect, and throwing off from her freshening limbs the death-shade and the grave clothes which had so long enshrouded her, ascended to the glorious resurrection of that noontide luster which irradiates the horizon of our own day, "rejoicing like a strong man to run a race."

Now some of these events paved the way for others —some were rendered useful solely from the previous existence of others, and all exerted upon each a reciprocal effect.

Among the fruits of this new order of things—of these new developments of mind—of this fresh impulse to the spirit of universal investigation, of which that cluster of great events was partly the cause and partly the effect, we should always give a prominent place to that department of knowledge called "*Physical Science.*" For although the middle of the fifteenth century is generally marked as the great era of the revival of religion and of letters, it is no less deserving of being distinguished as the time in which men began to study, appreciate, and comprehend the laws and phenomena of the material world; and it is a remarkable historical fact, that at the very time Martin Luther effected the revolution of the theological system, at Wittenberg, in a city sixty miles to the north, Nicholas Copernicus was revolutionizing the long-received system of astronomy. While the one taught that the "Seven-hilled City" was not the center of the Church, the other demonstrated that this world was not the center of the universe: glorious coincidence of great events—the type and the prophecy of the approaching emancipation of *Matter* and of *Mind!*

My theme is the present position and aspect of the Physical Sciences.

1. The Physical Sciences, previous to the fifteenth century, were the main agents and hand-maids of superstition.

Instead of contributing to the happiness of the race,

as they were then understood and wielded, they were the chief source of human disquietude and suffering.

The mass of men, ignorant of the laws which govern the material world, and hence wholly incompetent to unravel their mysteries and explain their phenomena, became the sport of every strange fact or uncommon occurrence which nature presented. The sudden appearance of an eclipse, or of a comet with its blazing tail, the coruscations of the Aurora Borealis, the explosion of subterranean gases, the bursting up of volcanic fires, the ignis fatuus, dancing over the marshy meadow at nightfall, have often filled whole nations with alarm.

Nor in those cases where a solution of these physical facts was known to a few more gifted than their fellows were the masses the wiser or the better. For such knowledge was hoarded up with jealous care—became the exclusive property of the mysterious alchymist—the cunning priest, the ambitious ruler, and was held in terror over the heads of the multitude.

And it is a subject of curious investigation, to trace out the mode in which science thus became an instrument in the hands of the *few*, to overawe and enslave the *many*. And we believe that history will bear us out in the assertion, that every known branch of physical science was laid under contribution to sustain some one species of religious and political imposture.

How often did a knowledge of the principles of Astronomy enable the general on the eve of battle, to calculate the time of an approaching eclipse, and attacking the enemy at the moment darkness was spreading over the earth, decide the contest in his own favor, by appealing to this visible interposition of the gods. Did not Archimedes, by his knowledge of Mechanics, toss the Roman ships in the air? or consume them with his burning lenses, thus arming Syracuse with protection more terrible than a wall of fire?

The Egyptian priests, by some secret art resembling our modern mesmerism, could charm the adder, and the serpent, and thus rivet the chains of ghostly power upon the necks of the people. In a word, what constituted the hidden mysteries of the ancient sorcerer, the physician, the astrologer? Nothing but a knowledge of a few chemical, astronomical, or herbal secrets, as familiar now as the letters of the alphabet. Doubtless the *secret use* which the ancients made of their scientific discoveries, has prevented many of their inventions from reaching our day: as for instance, the Egyptian art of embalming their dead, and the erection of the pyramids. Yet an examination of most of their famous miracles and fables will show us that their chief deceptions had their origin in physical science.

"The science of *acoustics* furnished the ancient sorcerers with some of their best deceptions. The imitation of thunder in their subterranean temples could not fail to indicate to a superstitious worshiper, the presence of a supernatural agent. The golden virgins, whose charming voices resounded through the temple of Delphos,—the stone from the river Pactolus, whose trumpet notes frightened the robber from the treasure which it guarded; the speaking head which uttered its oracular responses at Lesbos; the vocal statue of Memnon, which began at break of day to accost the rising sun in strains of melody; were all deceptions, derived from science, and from an imitation of the phenomenona of nature."

The principles of *Hydrostatics* were equally available in the work of popular deception. The marvelous fountain, which Pliny describes, in the island of Andros, as discharging wine for seven days, and water during the rest of the year; the spring of oil, which broke out at Rome, to welcome the return of Augustus from the Cicilian war; the empty urns which filled themselves with wine at the annual bacchanalian feasts in the city of Elis; the weeping statues, and the perpetual lamps in the old Greek and Roman temples; were all the effects of the equilibrium and pressure of fluids, known to the initiated, but hid from the vulgar.

The department of Mechanics, also, lent its aid. In the Eleusinian mysteries of ancien Rome, when the unfortunate victim was carried off by the gods, there is reason to believe that he was hurried away by the aid of machinery concealed in their temples.

When Appolonius, conducted by the Indian sages to the sanctuary of their deity, felt the earth rising and sinking beneath his feet, like the agitated sea, he was doubtless placed upon a moving floor, made to imitate the heaving of the waves.

The rapid descent of those who consulted the oracle in the cave of Trophonius; the walking statues of Antium; the wooden pigeons of Archytas; yea, almost all the pretended miracles of antiquity, are specimens of the mechanical resources of ancient magic.

But, doubtless, the science of *Optics* was the main dependence in the ancient arts of deception. The power of bringing remote objects apparently within the very grasp of the observer, and swelling into gigantic magnitude objects the most minute, never fails to inspire with astonishment even those who know something of the process by which such marvels are accomplished. What then must have been their effect upon the minds of the ignorant? The ancients, indeed, were not acquainted with those combinations of lenses and mirrors which constitute the modern telescope and microscope, but they possessed the power of distorting, inverting, and even of igniting objects by means of plates of polished steel; and in many of the descriptions of the optical displays which hallowed their temples, we recognize all the transformations of the modern *phantasmagoria* (See Brewster's Letters).

Now, when we contemplate these facts, how wonderful the change in the aspect and use of the physical sciences! How has the right arm of superstition been broken? How has the giant been shorn of his strength and laid harmless at our feet? and man can now walk abroad, and gaze upon nature in all her external displays or hidden wonders, unawed, unterrified.

2. Another new aspect which the physical sciences have assumed, and in which they differ from what they were in former ages, is their *diffusion*. Once they well deserved the name of *Occult Sciences;* for they were secrets known only to the *few*—sacred mysteries veiled from the vulgar. They were like light upon the mountain top, while the valleys were wrapped in darkness—fountains in high places, whose streams sent down a penurious supply to the plains below.

The custom, ever since the revival of learning, of writing all scientific works in the Latin language (a language unknown to the people); the scarcity and high price of books; the want of philosophical instruments, in connection with the warlike habits of the world—all conspired to render science, for many ages, a *monopoly*, and confined it to the call of the monk, and the dusty garret of the alchymist. But now the spell is dissolved. Nature has thrown wide her doors, has revealed her hidden wonders, and *all men* are invited to enter and worship at her shrine.

The physical sciences received their first great impulse from the art of printing, fostered by the universal inquisitiveness and adventurous spirit which that art created. Next came the labors of Lord Bacon (the greatest genius, in many respects, which England ever produced), who pointed out the only true mode of philosophizing. Then came the discoveries of Galileo, Kepler, and Newton; and finally, about the middle of the last century, there began to issue from the press a large number of popular works on natural history, geography, astronomy, and experimental philosophy; and these, divested of the pedantry of former times, and the technicalities of the old philosophy, began to operate on the mass, and transferred knowledge from the *few* to the *many*—from the pampered priest and feudal lord, to the peasant and mechanic. And thus, in process of time, a new order of things has arisen. A new era in the age of the world has dawned. And now the arts and sciences are like the light of the sun, or the showers that burst from the clouds, or the broad surface of rivers and seas; the birthright and blessing of *all men;* and, guided by the light of a few simple principles, multitudes in the humbler walks of life, who would once have been spurned as unworthy to set their unhallowed feet upon the threshold of the temple of science, are astonishing the world by their inventions and discoveries. Verily "many are running to and fro, and knowledge is increased."

3. Another remarkable aspect of the physical sciences, and in which they differ essentially from what they once were, is their *practical tendency;* their every day utility; their adaptedness to the actual state of things; affording direct alleviation to the physical and social wants of man.

The age of theories and day-dreams is no more. The time when men shut themselves up, and exhausted both mind and body with learned trifles, and spun out fine cobwebs of the brain, of no practical benefit to themselves or others, has passed away never to return.

How humiliating to contemplate the follies of the ancient school-men; the utter destitution in their most profound disquisitions of anything like *practical utility*. Yea, it would seem that the greatest *philosophers* were the greatest *fools*, and that the higher they advanced in their fancied learning, the farther they receded from common sense. "Men," says Lord Bacon, "withdrew themselves from the contemplation of Nature, and tumbled up and down, in their own fancies and conceits. They sought truth in their own little world, and not in the great and common world" around them.

Behold a conclave of grave fathers of the Church, laboring with holy fervor and orthodox zeal, to determine,—whether God can exist as well in *imaginary* space as in *real* space; whether God loves a non-existing angel more than an existing insect; whether angels can see in the dark; whether an angel can pass from one point of space to another, without passing through the intermediate space. Is it not such "stuff that dreams are made of?" Equally absurd were the trifles which absorbed the attention of the student of *physical science*. Look at one toiling from youth to hoary age to find out the philosopher's stone; another, the secret of transmuting all metals into gold; a third is bent upon the perpetual motion; a fourth tortures Nature to extract from her a universal medicine, by which to cure all earthly diseases and rejuvenate the powers of man; while a fifth consults the stars to foretell coming events, and cast the horoscope of kings.

"They could foretell whatever was
By consequence to come to pass—
As death of great men, alterations,
Diseases, battles, inundations;
They would search a planet's house to know
Who broke and robbed a house below;

Examine Venus and the moon,
Who stole a thimble or a spoon;
They would question Mars, and, by his looks,
Detect who 'twas that soiled your books;
They'd feel the pulses of the stars,
To find out agues, coughs, catarrhs;
And all earth's mysteries unriddle,
As easily as you can thread a needle."—*Hudibras.*

But now this age of learned folly, of wise ignorance, of sublime nonsense, has passed forever away, and been succeeded by an age of *practical utility*.

And now can be realized, in some good degree, another beautiful sentiment of the great Lord Bacon: "Men no longer seek in knowledge a *couch*, whereon to rest a searching and restless spirit; nor a *terrace*, for a wandering mind to walk up and down, with a fair prospect; nor a *tower of state*, for a fond mind to raise itself upon; nor a *fort* or *commanding ground*, for strife and contention; nor a *shop*, for profit and sale; but a *rich storehouse*, for the glory of the Creator and the good of man's estate."

We set out by attempting to account for all the strange facts and phenomena of antiquity, upon some well-known principle of physical science. We think we have explained a *few*, but there are *some* which are too profound for our philosophy. For instance, Mercatus, physician to Philip II. of Spain, relates that he actually saw a beautiful lady break a steel mirror to pieces, and peel the bark off some trees, by a single glance of her eyes! Josephus relates that a certain Jew, named Eleazer, in the presence of the Emperor Vespasian, drew the devil out of an old woman's nostrils by the application of Solomon's seal to her nose! Good old Dr. Mynsight is said to have cured several bewitched persons with a plaster of assafœtida. How the assafœtida was efficacious was much disputed among the learned. Some thought the devil might consider such an application to any part an insult, and ran off in a passion. But others very sagely observed that, as devils are supposed to have eyes and ears, they doubtless have noses also, and dislike vile smells to come between the wind and their olfactories. But let us drop this point, lest we suffer in the conflict. It is dangerous to meddle with devils and witches.

They'll haul you o'er the coals,
And stir the fires of Phlegethon,
With every mother's son;
Nor say one single mass,
To cool the caldron's bubble,
That boils your bones—
Unless you pay them double.

We repeat the remark, that every branch of physical science is now cultivated, primarily, for the sake of *utility*. "*Cui bono*" is the motto of every philosopher. Behold *Astronomy* taking up her instruments, and making an actual measurement of the magnitude and distances of the heavenly bodies, explaining their influences and variations, and even measuring the comet in its swift and fiery flight. The moon has struck and come under our lee, that we may gaze upon her burning mountains. The little star, which seems no bigger than the diamond that glitters on a lady's ring, is really found to be the center of a magnificent system, around which vast worlds revolve.

View *Meteorology*, explaining the laws of the clouds, and the philosophy of storms, for the benefit of the farmer, the mariner, and the fisherman.

Geology searches amid primeval rocks, and the dry beds of old oceans, to furnish man with a knowledge of shells and soils and metals.

Natural History unfolds, for practical purposes, the properties and uses of beasts, insects, and birds.

Botany takes man by the hand, and leads him out into the green fields, to teach him the uses of plants and roots and flowers.

Chemistry stands behind her retorts and crucibles, and discourses of earths and alkalies and gases, teaching man how to compound medicines, prepare food, improve soils, burnish metals, manufacture glass, disinfect impure habitations, and bleach and dye garments.

And what shall we say of *Mechanics?* Calling to her aid a few of the simple principles of nature and art, and pressing them into her service, she has given the world the mariner's compass, the safety-lamp, the diving-bell, the air-pump, the microscope, the spinning-jenny, the lightning-rod, the magnetic needle, the electric telegraph. Such are her rich gifts to man.

And what shall we say of the practical application of science in the wonders of *Steam?* Oh, this is the lever by which we are moving the world. It has armed the feeble hand of man with a power to which no limits can be assigned, completed the dominion of mind over matter, and is causing old things to pass away and all things to become new. Men have dug down mountains and crossed oceans by steam. The Birmingham fire-king has visited the fabulous East, and the genius of the Cape has been alarmed at the thunders of his voice. The shuttle drops from the fingers of the weaver, and falls into iron fingers that can move it faster. The horse is stripped of its harness, and finds a fleet fire-horse yoked in its stead. The sailor has folded his sails, to bid a strong, unwearied servant to bear him on vapory wings over the waters. "The Allegheny has bowed down his back like a camel to receive the load of commerce; and the waters have gone over him, and the navies of boats ride in triumph over his high places." Nature, through all her works, has surrendered. The victory of mind is achieved. Even distance has been annihilated, and, panic-struck, has vanished from St. Anthony to New Orleans; and the panic is spreading, and distance, in all directions, is fleeing away. If such are the achievements of Science in her infancy, what will she not achieve when arrived at manhood? when other Newtons, and Arkwrights, and Fultons, and Morses shall arise, with minds still more brilliantly illuminated with the lights of science, and the splendid achievements of the present age shall be far surpassed by the future miracles of mechanic power.

4. We should be doing violence to our own feelings, and injustice to our subject, were we to omit to point out another prominent characteristic of physical science. It is the fact that it is confirmatory of revelation. It is becoming the direct *auxiliary of Christianity*. And every new fact and development is only adding to that great cloud of witnesses which attest the divinity of our holy religion. Once it was not so. Once science was viewed with suspicion. Once it was discountenanced because of its supposed contrariety to the principles of the Gospel. The inventor of the art of printing was thought to be in league with the devil. Galileo was cast into the dungeons of the Inquisition, for teaching that the sun is stationary and the earth moves around it. Columbus was opposed in his theory of the globular shape of the world, and of a western passage to the Indies, by its alleged inconsistency with revelation. But a short time has elapsed since geology was looked upon as subversive of the whole Mosaic narrative. But now how changed the whole aspect of the scientific world. Our men of wisdom are becoming men of God. Every science and every system is now bringing its offering, to

lay them at the foot of the cross. Science and Revelation walk hand in hand, the one as the queen, the other as the queen-daughter by her side. And the missionary of salvation, as he goes far hence to enlighten the teeming millions of the East, has only to teach the first principles of *physical science,* and many of the systems of heathenism begin to crumble, and their idols totter to the ground. Glorious aspect of the sign of the times. The revelations of nature are in harmony with the revelations of Scripture. And future Lockes, placing it above all philosophy; and Bacons, above all learning; and Newtons, above all science; and Miltons, above all song—each bearing his precious gift—shall come, like Eastern magi, with their gold, their frankincense and myrrh, and lay them in lowly worship at the feet of the Prince of Peace.

I call upon the devotee of science to contemplate this noble and sublime aspect of revealed religion. It is the great fixed point around which all things else revolve, while itself remains unchanged. It is the emblem of Him who gave it, the all-embracing medium, in which every other thing moves, increases, or lessens, is born and destroyed. It is the last refuge of thought, the binding link between the visible and invisible. It is the solution of all anomalies, the determination of all problems in outward nature and in the inward soul. It is the fixing and steadifying element of every system, the grand object of every meditation. It appears to us even as the olive, that emblem of peace and duration, as described by Sophocles; a plant not set by human hands, but of spontaneous and necessary growth, in the great order of creative wisdom; fearful to its enemies, and so firmly grounded that none, in ancient or modern times, have been able to uproot it. Yea, it is a monument, standing in the solitude of the desert, upon which is inscribed the history of men and nations, which for ages rose and flourished, and then burst like bubbles at its base. It is a rock in the ocean of time, which has braved the fury of a thousand storms. It has withstood the plots of politicians, the revolutions of empires, the gloom of the dark ages, the sophistry of infidels, the fires of martyrdom, and the rage of devils.

In concluding this imperfect sketch of the present aspect and practical tendencies of the physical sciences, we shall detain the audience with only one reflection. This subject teaches the transcendent importance of fostering schools and colleges. The discoveries of the past must be carefully transmitted to the future. And what shall be the medium? Let the great Lord Bacon answer. "Our duty towards learning," says he, "is conversant about three objects—the places of learning, the books of learning, and the persons of the learned. For as water, whether it be of the dew of heaven, or the springs of the earth, doth scatter and lose itself in the ground, except it be collected into some receptacle, where it may, by union, comfort and sustain itself; and for that cause the industry of man hath made and framed spring-heads, conduits, cisterns, and pools, which men have accustomed likewise to beautify and adorn; so this excellent liquor of knowledge, whether it descends from divine inspiration or springs from human sense, would soon perish and vanish to oblivion, if it were not preserved in books, traditions, conferences, and places appointed; as universities, colleges, and schools, for the receipt and comforting of the same." Let all, then, who are engaged in founding institutions of learning, be encouraged by the fact that they are forming spring-heads and pools to collect and preserve "this excellent liquor of knowledge." Not all the luster of a noble birth, not all the influence of wealth or fame, not all the pomp of titles, not all the splendor of power, not all the joys of carnal pleasure, not all the charms of beauty, can impart such dignity to the soul, or so assimilate man to the angels, as this. This will grow, while all else decays. This will cling to us, while all else forsakes. This will survive, while the grandest works of genius and of art will expire amid the universal wreck of matter and of worlds. Colleges will outlive empires.

DUELING IN VICKSBURG.

ABOUT the time of the removal of the Indians from North Mississippi to the Indian Territory, west of the river, Vicksburg began to assume the appearance of a city. On my arrival from Louisiana to take the pastoral charge of the Presbyterian Church in that place, in the Fall of 1836, I beheld a most animated scene. The eye of the stranger was greeted by the sight of a most brilliant panorama—crowded streets, thronged wharfs, well-filled warehouses, and a large and bustling population. Every man seemed to be a man of business. Multitudes were running to and fro. The countenances of all beamed with hope, the hearts of all beat high with joyous expectation. Crowds of Virginians and Kentuckians, with their families and slaves, were pouring in from every steamer; and from this city of the bluffs, as from a hill of observation, multitudes were selecting fresh homes on the Sunflower, the Yazoo, and other portions of the vast territory offered for sale, by the withdrawal of the red men to the further west. New streets were opening, scores of new dwellings were in process of erection, and every corner rang with the noise of the saw and the hammer. Property of all kinds in Vicksburg rose to a fabulous height; and hotels were crowded to such a degree as to make it necessary to portion out, by *chalk-marks* on the floor, designated spots where strangers might lie down and repose for the night. Physicians and lawyers and land speculators were innumerable. No city in the South was more attractive than Vicksburg. Every man was going to Vicksburg. Every speculator was buying lots in Vicksburg. Soon, however, the scene was changed. That melancholy pecuniary revulsion which, in 1838, came upon the whole commercial world, spread like a funeral pall over the young city. The hum of business began to die away. The wheels of industry moved sluggishly. The sinews of trade were cut; and ere long every citizen experienced the effects of a wide-spread embarrassment. And soon, from loss of confidence and loss of trade, from fires and epidemics, Vicksburg became but the shadow of its former self. Its wealth had taken to itself wings like an eagle, and had fled. The gay and busy multitude that once thronged its streets had faded away. They slept their last sleep on the bleak hillside after life's fitful fever was over. "Lord, what is man! His days are as grass. As a flower of the field, so he flourisheth. For the wind passeth over it, and it is gone; and the place thereof shall know it no more, forever."

Let us take a brief glance at another "picture from life in Vicksburg." We pass over the years of 1838 and 1839, down to 1840. But the gloomy fall of 1841, who can forget it, who can describe it? It was the great *yellow fever* year. If an invading army had suddenly burst upon the town, the panic could not have been more terrible or the effects more desolating. Disease and death entered almost every dwelling. For six long weeks we bore the dead to the grave in almost one continuous stream. The shafts of the pestilence flew thick and fast. And the fairest were the first to fall. The maiden was cut down in her bloom and beauty, the young man in the midst of his pleasures; the old man and the man of influence, the learned counselor and the eloquent orator. Death tore away the props of families, removed the ornaments of the State, broke down the pillars of the church, and clad our city in lamentation and woe, leaving behind weeping widows and desolate orphans. Then, upon a damp and chilly Sabbath morning in November, with a heart almost broken with the afflictions of the people, I staggered to the church, and in the audience of sixty-four men (all told), and not a female in the house, I spoke from these words of St. Paul: "But this I say, brethren, the time is short. It remaineth that both they that have wives be as though they had none; and they that weep, as though they wept not; and they that rejoice, as though they rejoiced not; and they that buy, as though they possessed not; and they that use this world, as not abusing it, for the fashion of this world passeth away."

Turn over to another tragedy in the Walnut Hill city. Vicksburg had been, for some years before the season of yellow fever, the seat of the gamblers. The formidable gang of the Murell men, which had pervaded the entire State, had been dispersed. Murell, their ringleader, had been incarcerated in the penitentiary at Nashville, and hordes of horse-thieves and negro-stealers had been broken up. Then another formidable cloud arose. Fierce and lawless men, but of polished manners, who had been increasing in numbers and power in the young city of Vicksburg, had attracted the notice of the people of the great South, and had even called down the animadversions of members of the British Parliament. Gamblers ruled the day. Gambling-tables had usurped the place of law and set peaceful citizens at defiance. Suddenly the mass of quiet and law-abiding men, who loved their property and their families, arose in their armed majesty, and, after the outlaws had killed Dr. Bodley, they seized the ringleaders, put some on flatboats and set them adrift on the

Mississippi, and dragging five of the remaining number to a neighboring hill, improvised a long gallows, hung them by the neck until they were dead, and buried them in unhallowed graves.

Then, for a time, the place had peace. Next arose the reign of the duello. Almost "every man had his little game." Every one had his duel. Rival lovers had their duel. Almost every dispute was settled by a duel. Foote and Prentiss had their duel. Hagan and McCardle had their duel. There were duels of pastime and duels of etiquette. Aikenhead and Flaherty fought about the right mode of preparing Irish potatoes for the dinner-table. Chilton and Harris left the Odd Fellow's lodge when in session, crossed the river, and fought. General Foote and S. S. Prentiss had another awkward duel; and so crooked was the general's firing, that Prentiss cried out to the little boys on the trees that overhung the ground, "Boys, look out, or you will be hit. General Foote can't shoot straight. He has missed me three times." Lastly, there were some who became celebrated surgeons or famous seconds to duels. Dr. Green was tall and gaunt. He seemed to me far above six feet high, solemn and grim at that:

> "The fiend was long, and lean, and lank,
> And moved upon a spindle shank."

But because of his skill in loading rifles for duels, Prentiss dubbed him "Death's ramrod."

Thus, from grave to gay, swung the popular current.

The last serious affair of the kind, to which I would now advert, was the celebrated duel between Col. A. K. McClung and Major Menifee, opposite the city, in November, 1838. Col. McClung was a nephew of Chief Justice Marshall, was a famous duelist, skilled to perfection in deadly weapons, had killed Col. Allen, of

Brandon, and, after many rencounters of the kind, finally committed suicide. A challenge was passed and accepted between the parties. Great preparations were made. Fresh dueling weapons were ordered from New Orleans. Sporting men came in crowds from Jackson, Brandon, and the interior towns. Bets were freely made and accepted. The hills around the fatal spot were covered with thousands of spectators. At the hour appointed the parties took their position, the word was given, the parties fired, and Menifee fell. McClung fled to the interior. Major Menifee was buried on Friday.

On the following Sabbath morning a crowd assembled at the Presbyterian Church, when the writer, who had been preparing a discourse for the occasion, arose and spoke as follows

THE CODE OF HONOR.

"*Thou shalt not kill.*"—Exodus 20:13. This prohibitory enactment of heaven, was designed to be of universal application; forbidding the taking, not merely the life of man, but likewise of beast.

Before any one, therefore, can be innocent in taking life from any creature, whether rational or irrational, he must first obtain express permission from the same high authority from which this law originally emanated. Such permission, has, in some few particular cases, been obtained. Thus God expressly gave to Noah and his sons permission to destroy the lives of animals and use their flesh as food. And this grant contains our only warrant for the taking of animal life.

If, then, we may not take the lives of animals without express permission from the King of heaven, much less may we take away the life of *man*—God's noblest work, made in his own image, constituted Lord of Creation, endowed with reason, and heir of immortality.

Has God specified any cases where the life of man may be taken? He has. The Scriptures, in several places and in a variety of forms, declare that human life may be lawfully destroyed in righteous warfare between two nations; by the civil magistrate as a punishment for murder, and in necessary self-defence. With these three exceptions, the Scriptures are most solemn and fearful in their denunciations of divine wrath and indignation against the destruction of human life under any other circumstances.

The prohibition of the text therefore—"*thou shalt not kill*"—is aimed directly against all acts of violence offered to man which are not included under these three specified exceptions, *i. e.*, it is aimed against *murder*, *suicide*, and *dueling*. I call your attention to the latter crime.

Dueling is a crime of very great prevalence, upheld by many plausible arguments, and sometimes practiced or countenanced by individuals of high respectability, and in some respects of much moral worth.

What are the arguments against it?

1. Its very origin and history condemns it. Dueling was entirely unknown among the ancient Greeks and Romans. The polished Greek knew nothing of it; the noble Roman was above it. The custom is exclusively of a heathenish and savage origin. It arose among the fierce and warlike nations of the north of Europe. The ancient Germans, Danes, and Franks, carried this mode of warfare so far, that none were excused, except women, sick persons, cripples, and those over sixty years of age. Even ecclesiastics and monks were required to decide many of their contests by an appeal to single combat.

Bear in mind, however, that the object and design of contest by *duel*, among those northern barbarians, was very different and far more rational, than the duel of modern times.

The object of the ancient duel was to decide important points relative to crime or property. Criminal accusations, or titles to landed estates, were always the subjects of dispute. And the trial by duel was a species of high court of appeals. It was considered as a direct reference of the whole matter to God, the great arbiter of right; who, it was believed, would always decide the contest by terminating it in favor of the innocent party; and then the party vanquished, if not slain upon the spot, was punished by hanging, beheading, or mutilation of members.

But the design of the modern duel is vastly different. *Its* object is to decide, not the titles to property, or accusations of crime, but points of honor—points of such a delicate and invisible character, that half the world have never yet been able to perceive them, or determine in what they consist.

The modern duel, or the duel upon points of honor, may be dated as far back as the year 1528, when Charles V., emperor of Germany, challenged Francis I. of France, by a public herald, accompanied by the graceful epithets of coward, liar, poltroon, etc. From that period it became customary, throughout Europe, whenever a gentleman received an insult or injury which seemed to touch his honor, he thought himself entitled immediately to draw his sword and demand satisfaction. Dueling became so common in France, that it is calculated that six thousand persons perished in single combat, during ten years of the reign of Henry IV. The effusion of human blood from the same cause, was frightfully prevalent in England during the time of James I. and the two Charleses. And what is the history of this bloody code of honor in our own land?

Within the last half century of our political existence, how often has our land been clad in mourning? How often have we yielded up the most costly victim to glut the maw of this bloody Moloch? Hamilton, and Decatur, and Cilley, and a host of others, both of our army and navy, the pride of many a rising family, our country's strength in war, its ornaments in peace,—Oh "how are the mighty fallen!" How have the most valuable lives been sacrificed, and the most precious blood been spilt, in conformity to a custom which knows no origin but superstition, no reason but madness, no apology but revenge! And the practice is still gaining ground, with all its attendant curses,—such as the dishonorable and cowardly practice of carrying concealed weapons, making a man an offender for a word—bloody broils and street fights—a disposition to decide every contest, except that relating to property, by a resort to the pistol or the dagger. Even our sacred halls of legislation have been the scene of bloody strife. Alas, our land is soaked in gore, and calls on God for vengeance. The very history of dueling then, with its attendant evils, proclaims its condemnation and brands it with infamy.

2. Dueling is a direct violation of all the settled principles of law, both human and divine.

In Genesis, 9: 6, God thus declares: "Whoso sheddeth man's blood, by man shall his blood be shed; for in the image of God made he man."

In Numbers, 35 : 16, etc., it is thus written—if a man smite any person "with an instrument of iron, so that he die," he is a murderer; "the murderer shall surely be put to death." And if he smite him "with a hand weapon of wood, wherewith he may die, and he die, he is a murderer; the murderer shall surely be put to death." "Whoso killeth any person, the murderer shall be put to death by the mouth of witnesses." "Moreover, ye shall take no satisfaction for the life of a murderer who is guilty of death, but he shall surely be put to death." "The land cannot be cleansed of the blood shed therein but by the blood of him that shed it." Such is the law of God. Equally explicit are the laws of man. What says Blackstone, Book IV., ch. 14? "If two persons, A and B, agree to fight a duel, and A gives the first onset, and B retreats as far as he safely can, and then kills A, this is murder, because of the previous malice and concerted design." Again says the same authority: "Killing must be committed with *malice aforethought* to make it the crime of murder." "This takes in the case of deliberate dueling, where both parties meet avowedly with an intent to murder, thinking it their duty as gentlemen, and claiming it as their right to wanton with their own lives and those of their fellow creatures, without any warrant or authority from any power, either divine or human, but in direct contradiction to the laws of both God and man; and, therefore, the law has justly fixed the crime of punishment of murder on them, and their seconds also."

What says Dr. Paley? "Murder is forbidden, and wherever human life is deliberately taken away, otherwise than by public authority, there is murder."

What says Mr. Russell, in his treatise on crimes? "A party killing another in a deliberate duel is guilty of murder, and cannot help himself by alleging that he was first struck by the deceased, or that he had often declined to meet him, and was prevailed upon to do so by his importunity, or that it was his intent only to vindicate his reputation, or that he meant not to kill, only to disarm his adversary. He has deliberately engaged in an act highly unlawful, and he must abide the consequences."

Such is the law of England. The laws of almost every commonwealth in the United States are equally explicit. In Vermont, for killing in a duel, it is death. In Massachusetts it is the same. In Rhode Island, for fighting, although death may not ensue, the punishment is carting to the gallows, with a rope about the neck, and sitting on the gallows an hour, and subsequent imprisonment. In Maryland and Virginia, it is political disfranchisement. What is the law of Mississippi? The challenger, or bearer of a challenge, is prohibited from holding any office of trust, and is liable to six months' imprisonment, and a fine of one thousand dollars.

All justices of the peace are required to give testimony against duelists, and the survivors in a duel required to pay the debts of the man killed.

But here is a code of laws, setting at naught all these sacred enactments both of earth and heaven. Coming out like Goliath of Gath, and defying the authority of the living God.

3. Dueling is murder, and that too of the most aggravated and enormous character, and it is murder, not merely where the death of one of the parties ensues. For the common law declares that if one man attempts the life of another and fails in the attempt, he is a murderer, and should be punished accordingly. Look, too, at the many additional circumstances, which constitute every duel, whether resulting fatally or not, the most *heaven-daring* murder.

It is premeditated murder; for every challenge contains a proposition to kill or be killed. It is accepted always with the express expectation of killing or being killed. It is deliberate murder; for days and even weeks often elapse previous to the contemplated meeting. In the meantime weapons are prepared, and that too of the most deadly character. Previous practicing takes place. Friends are chosen. The spot is marked out. Witnesses are present. The broad light of heaven beams down upon the guilty scene; and then, all things being ready, the most deliberate aim is taken at the seat of life—the head, the heart, and the lungs.

Can any murder be conceived of a more atrocious character than this? Does the highwayman or the assassin commit murder under circumstances half so aggravating? Murder, then, is committed in duels with ten-fold more deliberation than murder under any other circumstances, and murder is here committed without any adequate cause. "Trifles light as air," causes the most contemptible and silly, a rash word, a disrespectful look, an indiscreet remark, dropped in the heat of debate, the clashing claims of rival lovers, party politics, petty envy—oh! these are the causes for which men expose their blood, and rush upon the bosses of Jehovah's buckler.

But it is said that the duelist feels *no malice;* that he fights merely for the point of honor. Neither does the highwayman feel *malice.* He who cuts the throat and rifles the pocket of the passing traveler, feels no malice; and if he could procure his money at a less costly price, would stay his murderous hand and let the trembling victim off. But what says the common law relative to this thing of killing without malice? It declares where one man assails another with a deadly instrument with an intent to kill, malice is implied. For if he have not a particular malice, he entertains a general malice—a malice against all mankind—an innate thirst for blood, which renders him unfit to live. But we deny that the duelist is free from particular malice.

Duels are generally the result of the most deliberate

malice; burning, diabolical malice; malice, which nothing will satisfy but the heart's blood.

Duelists, as a class, are preëminently haughty, irritable and revengeful, and to overlook an insult, that magnanimous act of a noble soul, is, in their view, the height of pusilanimity.

4. Dueling is suicide, as well as murder, and suicide may be committed not merely by one's own weapon, but by the weapon of another.

To permit another man deliberately to kill you, is the same as to commit the act yourself. Take away the circumstance of the duelist exposing his own life, and dueling becomes assassination. Add this circumstance and it becomes suicide. And who gave you authority to take away your own life, that most precious treasure, upon which such momentous interests depend? Your life is not your own. It belongs to your friends, your family, your creditors, your country. How dare you then, destroy that in which you do not possess an exclusive title? How dare you destroy that which was given you with which to work out your soul's salvation? Yea, the duelist puts himself upon an equality with the Lord Jesus Christ. Christ says, "I have power (or authority) to lay down my life." The duelist says "so have I!"

5. Dueling affords no reasonable prospect of securing the proposed end. The end or object proposed by the duelist is to gain satisfaction for some alleged insult, or to inflict punishment for some alleged crime. But how can the fighting a duel secure either satisfaction or punishment, seeing that the innocent is just as liable to fall as the guilty; seeing that the victim depends not upon the rectitude of the cause, but upon skill in the use of deadly weapons. Or, is the object of a duel to wipe off a disgrace, to repel a foul and infamous charge?

How can it possibly effect this object? How can smoke, and noise, and blood alter the nature of things? I am accused of being a liar, how can the firing of a pistol make me a man of truth? I am accused of being a villain and a knave, how can the same process prove the charge false, and make me an honorable man?

But absurd as it would seem to the dull comprehension of some of us, such is the magic power of an exchange of shots. According to the laws of honor, "it entirely varnishes over a defective and smutty character; transforms vice to virtue; cowardice to courage; makes falsehood, truth; guilt, innocence." In a word, it gives a new complexion to the whole state of things. The Ethiopian changes his skin, the leopard his spots; and the debauched and treacherous, having shot away the infamy of a sorry life, comes back from the field of perfectibility quite regenerated, and in the fullest sense, an honorable man. He is now fit for the company of "gentlemen." And let none dare dispute his title, or he will vindicate his tarnished honor by another act of homicide. Oh, what a cheap and expeditious mode of making gentlemen!

6. Dueling implies cowardice. Many brave men have fought, but their fighting was no part of their bravery. True, there may be courage, but it is only brute courage. Why is it that duelists often find such difficulty to screw their courage to the sticking point, and exhibit such woe-begone visages on the field of battle? Why so many wild and random shots?

But it is not the lack of physical courage for which we contend. The duelist lacks *moral courage.* He fights because he is afraid of public sentiment—afraid of being called a coward; he stands in awe of the sneers of the ungodly multitude. Who is the truly brave? He who conquers his corrupt passions. He who stems manfully the torrent of depraved public sentiment. He who dares to do what he knows to be right, and dares to abstain from what he knows to be wrong. But mark that little pusillanimous soul, violating his conscience, lest forsooth he may be called *a coward*—thus proving himself to be the very thing he would not have the world to think him!

7. Dueling, if it terminate fatally, damns the soul. "No murderer hath eternal life abiding in him."

In the case of suicide we may hope there was insanity. In the case of execution for murder, we may see previous exhibitions of genuine repentance. But what is our hope of him, who falls in the very act of defying the authority of the great Jehovah—dies a murderer—dies and goes to judgment—with blood upon his soul!

They turn'd him on his back; his breast
And brow were stain'd with gore and dust
And through his lips the life-blood oozed,
From its deep veins so lately loosed;
But in his pulse there was no throb,
Nor on his lips one dying sob;
Sigh, nor word, nor struggling breath
Heralded his way to death:
Ere his very thought could pray,
Unanel'd he pass'd away,
Without a hope from mercy's aid—
To the last a renegade.

8. Dueling is a most unjust and disproportioned code of iniquity. It inflicts the very same degree of punishment upon all offences indiscriminately. Death for a thoughtless word; and death for a deliberate act. Yea, it is a complete system of bullying. See with what instinctive sagacity this trained blood-hound selects his victim—always, if he can, insulting some one over whom he knows he has some advantage; and then dogging him from place to place to seek his blood. Oh, the

horrors of this bloody code of honor; trampling with fiendish cruelty upon all the sacred feelings of the heart; stained with the blood of statesmen, fathers, husbands; revelling in the groans of widows, the wail of orphans, the shrieks of sisters, lovers, friends!

> "—— Is there not some chosen curse,
> Some hidden thunder in the stores of heaven,
> Red with uncommon wrath, to blast the man
> Who gains his honor from the blood of souls?"

9. Dueling is condemned by the very confessions of duelists themselves. What bitter groans and regrets fell from the lips of Hamilton and Decatur! Observe the subsequent life and conduct of a successful duelist. Did you ever know such a man to be happy? Is he not pre-eminently miserable? afraid of being alone; plunging into one crime to avoid the reflection of another; drowning conscience in the intoxicating cup; and often becoming the victim of derangement. Then how conscience thunders and remorse goads; and the grim and gory ghost of the murdered one haunts him in his dreams! Oh, could he but drink of some oblivious stream and forget the past—forget that once he opened the fountain of the orphan's tears, and broke the widow's heart! But no, he cannot. Eternal justice will not suffer it. Oh! duelist, the remembrance of your deeds must follow you. Conscience will interpret everything into an accusation. When men fasten their eyes upon you, you will think they remember the man you murdered.

When men stand in groups and speak in whispers, you will imagine they are talking about you. Every work of God, and every deed of man will be to you an accuser. Oh, the horrors of blood-guiltiness! How it clings like a hungry vulture to the guilty soul!

"Though thy slumbers may be deep,
Yet thy spirit shall not sleep,
There are shades that will not vanish,
There are thoughts thou canst not banish;
By a power to thee unknown,
Thou canst never be alone.
By thy delight in others' pain,
By thy brotherhood of Cain,
I call upon thee and compel,
Thyself to be thy proper hell."

10. Dueling is subversive of all law and government. It saps the very foundations of civilized society; for it usurps the highest prerogatives of a nation: the right of taking away human life. The duelist takes upon himself the adjudication of his own wrongs, and thus lends his influence to resolve society into its original elements. All the laws of God and man must give way, while this man adjusts his quarrels. He must have the whole field of social, civil, and domestic relations subject to his fury. What though his enemy be a citizen charged with duty to the State; or a representative entrusted with the interest of his constituents; or a friend gladdening many a social circle; or a son sustaining and blessing fond and white-haired parents; or a husband cherishing a devoted, faithful wife; or a father, surrounded by affectionate, helpless children; what though he be all these and more—the claim of the duelist for his blood, on account of some unguarded or disrespectful word, is paramount to every other. God, and law, and nature, with all their sacredness, must be despised and trampled under foot, while this incarnation of ferocity gnashes his teeth, and gluts his maw, and quenches his fevered thirst for blood. And if he may act thus, why not his neighbor?

For what is right in one man, cannot be wrong in another. If *you* have a right to adjudicate your own quarrels, so have *I*. If *men* have, so have *boys*. And if you may kill your fellow-man for a word, why not for a deed? why not for a malicious prosecution, for disturbing your slumbers by a midnight riot, for bringing a contagious disease into your neighborhood and endangering the lives of your family? Oh, the long train of cause which follow in the train of this bloody god of honor! Every day our ears are made to tingle by tales of anarchy and violence, the brandishing of knives and pistols, the deeds of desperadoes and cut-throats, and all from what cause? Dueling is the cause of it.

Let us now briefly hear and answer some of the arguments of the duelist.

The duelist says that dueling, notwithstanding all that has been said against it, is necessary "as giving a man a passport among gentlemen." What a cheap way of making a gentleman! But are duelists more of gentlemen than their neighbors? Are they more honorable in their dealings, more punctual in the payment of their debts, and more attentive to all the courtesies of life than other men? Who generally fight duels? The blustering and the boisterous, bankrupts, gamblers, and upstarts—men often stained with a thousand crimes.

The duelist contends that the practice "has a tendency to make men polite and cautious in their remarks." Oh, it is making us polite savages, accomplished barbarians; causing men, from fear of some swaggering bully, to go armed to the teeth. Dueling, then, is producing the politeness of bandits and pirates. We are told that there are certain offences for which the law of the land provides no remedy, and, therefore, the duelist must fight. And what are these offences? Are they not generally the silliest trifles, fit only for children in the nursery? And where is the duelist's magnanimity, that he cannot pass over an insult? A gentleman *will not* insult you, a blackguard *cannot.*

We are told that it is the only way of avoiding the imputation of cowardice. You say, "How shall I avoid the imputation of cowardice unless I fight?" I would reply, if you do fight, how will you avoid the imputation of cruelty to your friends? of dishonesty to your creditors? of guilt to your conscience and your God? And if you fall, how will you avoid the damnation of hell? These are previous questions, which you are called upon to settle. Let your motto be, "I am not afraid to fight, but I am afraid to sin." And if you wish to show your courage, prosecute your challenger; defend your person, if he assails you; and help in voting out of office every officer who does not exert his authority in suppressing this vice, and in keeping the peace.

But the duelist says: "My character—my precious character has been assailed, and I must defend it." And what a frail thing your character must be, that a little breath of calumny can tarnish it. If your character is such a brittle thing as this, you had better get a better character—a firmer, stronger character. But the duelist says again: "I cannot bear up under the imputations cast upon my honor. I would rather die than bear it." Where is the duelist's vaunted courage? I thought duelists were all brave and heroic men. But it seems that a little charge breaks them down. They have not half the courage of many women. Others have been called liars and cowards, and still have survived the charge. And why may not these brave and fearless souls, by a few years of perseverance in the path of rectitude, silence every slander, and live down every imputation?

In conclusion, by all the solemn motives which can

operate upon a high-minded and generous community, I appeal to you—I call upon you as patriots, as heads of families, as lovers of peace, as friends of God—by all the sacredness of human life, by the law of your country, by the universal conscience of the civilized world; for the sake of our talented and chivalrous youth, on whom our country depends in war and in peace; by the silence of the dead; by the agony of surviving friends; by the anguish of widows, and the loneliness of orphans; by all the joys of heaven and hopeless misery of the lost, I adjure you to stay this foe to God and man. Let every freeman, and every man of moral courage, raise his voice in honest indignation; let the press speak out, and record every duel as a murder; let the lodge expel every Mason who fights; let candidates for office be required to abjure the bloody code; let every association which has for its object the amelioration of society, or the protection of property, frown upon the duelist, and drive him forth, a second Cain, with the brand of guilt burning on his brow—the stigma of murder fixed upon his name.

THE DIGNITY

OF THE

MINISTERIAL OFFICE.

Preached at the installation of Rev. J. J. Read, of Houston Church, Dec. 10, 1873.

"*I magnify mine office.*"—*Romans* 11 : 13. No man ever entertained a more exalted conception of the dignity of his office, than did the apostle Paul. With an intellect refined by all the culture of the age, with prospects of worldly eminence unsurpassed by any of his cotemporaries, he made of them a most willing sacrifice. Yea, doubtless he counted all things but loss that he might win Christ, and become a herald of his great salvation to the Gentile world. Acting on the principle suggested by sound philosophy, that no one can excel in any profession or pursuit in life, who does not entertain for it a most exalted conception, and engage in its duties with an ardor bordering on enthusiasm, he commenced a career of toil, of self-denial, and of suffering, of which the world cannot present a parallel. Hence, in every sacrifice he made, in every epistle he penned, in every church he founded, in every peril by land and sea which he endured—whether we view him standing before Felix, and reasoning with such overpowering majesty, as to cause that proud ruler to tremble, or as standing on Mars Hill, surrounded by the venerable court of the Areopagus, and there uttering terrible denunciations against those heathen gods, whose magnificent temples reared their stately columns all around him—one grand conception filled his soul, one master passion ruled his life, and that was, to "magnify his office"—to feel himself and make all around him feel, that he was clad with a vocation of all others the most honorable and the most important, worthy of his loftiest ambition, his most fervent zeal, his most unbounded efforts.

The text suggests the dignity and importance of the ministerial office.

1. This is shown from the honor which God has placed upon it in all ages of the world, and under all dispensations of the Church. God has but rarely communicated his will to earth, without the instrumental agency of man. Though sometimes he has made his purposes known by the medium of angels, by voices from the skies, by miracles, by solemn and significant ceremonies, by the peaceful rainbow, and the rumbling earthquake; yet it has ever been his chosen and most peculiar method to transmit his pleasure to earth by the lips of the living preacher, and the familiar and persuasive tones of the human voice. And although this chosen medium of divine communication is designated in Scripture by different appellations—though the men thus called by God are denominated Priests, Prophets, Preachers, or Seers,—yet the honor and the office have ever been substantially the same. Enoch, the seventh from Adam, was a prophet of the Lord, a public proclaimer of the will of heaven; and at last, in public attestation of his ministerial character and holy life, he was translated to heaven, that he should not see death. Noah also is denominated a preacher of righteousness; and during that long term of years in which he was preparing an ark for the saving of his house, he was oc-

cupied in publicly denouncing the sins of his time, and warning an ungodly world of its approaching doom. Abraham commanded his numerous household to serve the living God. Melchisedec was Prince of Salem, priest of the most high God, a glorious type of Christ, and published the glad news of future Gospel times. Moses was a most eminent publisher of heaven's will, deliverer, judge, ruler, and preacher—proclaimed the law of God from Mount Sinai, established the Jewish Church, and for forty years, his speech distilled like the dew upon the assembled congregations of God's chosen people. And thus, from Moses and Aaron to Solomon, Prince of Judah, and Amos, a herdsman of Tekoa, the noblest and most honored of all Israel's sons were public proclaimers of heaven's will. Some of these preachers delivered their messages in camps, and in courts, in deserts and on housetops. Some spoke to crowds, and some to individual auditors, as the Lord commanded. Sometimes they appeared in public with dishevelled hair and torn garments—with leathern girdles around their loins, and weapons of war in their hands, and yokes of slavery on their necks, and in various other methods by which to startle and alarm the people. They wept, and fasted, and prayed, and prophesied, and preached. There were schools of the prophets, seminaries for theological training, over which venerable men, such as Elisha, and Samuel, and others, presided. Behold Elijah, the Tishbite. He was an awful and solitary man. The divine afflatus came upon him, and tore him from the plow, and hurried him into the wilderness, where, communing with God and nature, he becomes qualified to be a reprover of kings, a denouncer of woe to a degenerate people. Then suddenly, as a vision of the night, he bursts upon King Ahab, delivers his message, and as suddenly disappears. Where is he?

We find him shortly after in a poor widow's dwelling, multiplying her handful of meal and cruse of oil, and raising her dead son to life. Again we see him upon the top of Mount Carmel, challenging the priests of Baal (four hundred and fifty), and the prophets of the groves (four hundred and fifty), to a public decision by fire, whether Baal be God, or Jehovah be God. Where is he now? He is at the brook Kishon, a heaven-constituted homicide, slaying the false prophets, heaps upon heaps. Now we find him compelling clouds and rain from the brazen sky and running before Ahab's chariot, to the entrance of Jezreel. We follow him again, a fugitive from Jezebel's vengeance, fleeing into the wilderness; fed by ravens; lodged in a cave; communing with God in the wind, in the earthquake, and the fire; and as he hears the still, small voice, he wraps his face in his mantle and bows his head, and worships. Again he sallies forth into the busy populace, armed with new terror, and burning to utter new messages; anoints Elisha as his successor; appears once more as a ghost to king Ahab; then turns his weary steps once more towards Jordan, with none but Elisha with him; smites the waters with his mantle; passes over dryshod; meets the fiery chariot let down from heaven; mounts the chariot like a king and conqueror; is carried upward in a whirlwind; drops his mantle; while Elisha stands awe-struck and cries after him, "My father, my father, the chariot of Israel and the horseman thereof." (See Gillfillan).

Pass now over a long sweep of years, and see what honor still clings to the heaven-constituted office of God's ministry, at a most important crisis in Jewish history. The Babylonish captivity, covering a period of seventy years, is drawing to its close. The captives of Israel, who had long hung their harps on the willows that skirted the streams of Babylon, and wept in silence when they remembered their distant homes, now lift up their heads with joy. The edict of Cyrus has gone forth—"Jerusalem shall be rebuilt—her altars re-established. Return, ye ransomed people, home." Then, at the grand re-organization of state and temple, behold God calling into prominent view his own chosen servants to do his own chosen work. What moral sublimity clusters around the person of Ezra, as, on the return of the people, he collects fifty thousand souls together near the water-gate, in the streets of Jerusalem. A pulpit of wood is erected above the heads of the immense mass, where, on elevated seats, on right and left, sat the Levites and elders of the people. As Ezra ascends the pulpit and opens the law, the whole mass, by a simultaneous impulse, rise and stand. As he offers up prayer and praise to God the people bow their heads and worship, with their faces to the ground; and at the prayer's close, with uplifted heads and hands, they respond, "Amen, amen."

Then the sermon begins—and what a sermon! For, as the preacher proceeds, every eye becomes a fountain of tears; and the elders weep; and the Levites weep; and all the people weep. And toward noon the weeping became so excessive and exhausting that the preacher and Levites had to restrain them. And in obedience to these wise and holy men, fifty thousand hearts are calmed in a moment, and they disperse in peace. Plato was alive at this very time, teaching cold philosophy to cold academies. But what was Plato, and what was Xenophon, and what was Demosthenes, in comparison with Ezra preaching at the water-gate, in the streets of Jerusalem?

From this period to the Christian era, public preaching was universal; synagogues were multiplied; vast numbers attended; and elders and preachers were appointed for the purpose of order and instruction. At last "came John the Baptist, preaching in the wilderness of Judea, and saying, repent ye; for the kingdom of heaven is at hand. For this is he that was spoken of by the prophet Esaias, saying, The voice of one crying in the wilderness, Prepare ye the way of the Lord, make his paths straight. And the same John had his raiment of camel's hair, and a leathern girdle about his loins; and his meat was locusts and wild honey. Then went out to him Jerusalem, and all Judea, and all the region round about Jordan. And were baptized of him in Jordan, confessing their sins."

But this bright "morning star" soon faded away before the rising splendor of the "glorious sun of righteousness," who spake as never man spake, and suffered as never man suffered, and died as never man died, and rose as never man rose; and forty days after his resurrection, led his disciples out as far as to Bethany, where he uttered his great commission: "Go ye into all the world and preach the Gospel to every creature; he that believeth and is baptized shall be saved, and he that believeth not shall be damned."

> "He spake and light shone round his head,
> On a bright cloud to heaven he rode;
> They to the farthest nations spread
> The faith of their ascending Lord."

2. The great dignity and honor of the ministerial office is shadowed forth by the many names and appellations by which it is designated in Holy Scripture. There is not an honorable epithet or title applied to occupations of distinction among men which is not used to illustrate the office of the ministry. Is the Church represented in Scripture under the similitude of a vineyard, ministers are the laborers toiling in its culture.

Is the church called a city, ministers are the watchmen stationed on its walls, to descry danger from afar and sound the alarm. Is the Church a sheepfold, they are the shepherds, guarding and feeding the flock. Is she a building, rising in fair proportions, eventually to be polished after the similitude of a palace, they are the builders rearing the gigantic and beauteous structure. Is Zion an army with banners, they are the standard-bearers. Is this world a revolted province of God's empire, they are the ambassadors, sent forth to adjust the claims of heaven's court and beseech men, in Christ's stead, to become reconciled to God. Is the Church on earth an object upon which the ascending Saviour wishes to bestow the richest boon, ministers are the precious donation. "Wherefore when he ascended up on high, he led captivity captive, and gave gifts unto men. And he gave some, apostles; and some, prophets; and some, evangelists; and some, pastors and teachers; for the perfecting of the saints, for the work of the ministry, for the edifying of the body of Christ: till we all come in the unity of the faith, and of the knowledge of the Son of God, unto a perfect man, unto the measure of the stature of the fulness of Christ." Would the enraptured Isaiah depict the future glories of the universal church, ministers form a prominent object in the glowing picture: "How beautiful upon the mountains are the feet of him that bringeth good tidings, that publisheth peace; that bringeth good tidings of good, that publisheth salvation; that saith unto Zion, Thy God reigneth! Thy watchmen shall lift up the voice; with the voice together shall they sing; for they shall see eye to eye, when the Lord shall bring again Zion."

3. The ministerial office assumes an aspect of vast dignity because of its rich fruits—its countless and transcendent blessings. Pen cannot recount, tongue

cannot utter, history will never adequately record the blessings which accompany and flow from the establishment of the Gospel ministry—diffusing themselves in ten thousand channels, over the Church and the world, over religion and science, over refinement and laws. Since the days of Christ and his inspired apostles, the *voice of the living preacher* has been the method the most conspicuous and the most honored of God in propagating the truth and conserving the world. For ever since that period, the chief function of the ministry consists in *preaching*, accompanied with prayer and the administration of the ordinances. There are no successors of the Jewish priests—there are no successors of the twelve apostles. The ministry now hath no sacerdotal or apostolic character. There are no lords over God's heritage. All God's ministers are equal. All are bishops, and all are brethren; and Christ alone is Head, and Christ alone is King. And in compensation for the withdrawal from the world of miraculous gifts, prophetic tongues, apostolic pens, and angels' visits, God has concentrated the essence of all former honors and offices upon the Christian ministy. Yea, there are clear intimations in Holy Scripture of God's design to circumscribe great spiritual blessings within its immediate range. "How, then (saith the apostle), shall they call on him in whom they have not believed; and how shall they believe in him of whom they have not heard; and how shall they hear without a preacher; and how shall they preach except they be sent." "So faith cometh by hearing, and hearing by the word of God." As true as God does not warm men without fire, nor nourish men without food, nor drown men without water, just so sure does he not usually convert men without preaching. Though there ever have been, and ever will be, cases of sincere conversion without the public preaching of the Gospel, yet they are of rare occurrence—exceptions to God's great rule. "The pulpit

> "Must stand acknowledged while the world shall stand,
> The most important and effectual guard,
> Support and ornament of virtue's cause."

What myriads of sacred influences and associations cluster around the pulpit, calculated to enhance its importance as a *moral power*. There is a vast element for good in having a class of men expressly set apart to instruct the people in holy things—with minds stored with learning—with hearts warm with love—with lips eloquent with truth—whose themes are divine—whose topics are the whole range of Bible facts—and whose arguments and motives are drawn from life and from death, from time and eternity. Look also at the influence of numbers, the power of sympathy, the expression of the human eye, the tones of the human voice, the whole force and magnetic power of human eloquence, calculated to awe, to thrill, to convince. Who can fully estimate the amount of knowledge communicated by the weekly ministrations of the Sanctuary, to a people many of whom are thoughtless and would never otherwise pause and reflect, and many are defective in education and incompetent to comprehend without a teacher? Who can recount the blessings to neighborhoods and villages in the instruction given, the impressions produced, the vices restrained, the public order upheld, and the peace, harmony, and friendships created by a regular ministry? And, on the other hand, what a melancholy scene presents itself to the eye, where there is no Christian ministry—in Sabbaths desecrated, public morals lowered, youth unrestrained, the Bible unread, and God and eternity forgotten—vice stalking abroad unrebuked, and the large mass grasping after wealth and pleasure, and no one to raise his voice and warn them to flee from the wrath to come.

And Oh, when we take a higher range—when we look upon the ministry as chiefly designed to proclaim to men a crucified Saviour, and qualify them for heaven, how the office swells in honor and dignity. And next to Jesus, the Lamb in the midst of the throne, the chief objects of interest and attraction in the upper state, will be those ministers of the Gospel, who have converted the largest number of souls to God. For "they that turn many to righteousness, shall shine as the stars forever and ever." Raphael took a piece of canvas, of which the maker thought nothing, and the vendor thought nothing, and threw upon it his own immortal colors, and has made it live forever in the galleries of Europe. So a minister of the Gospel takes a human heart, for which the possessor cares but little, and retraces upon it the lineaments of God's own image, to be exhibited forever in the galleries of heaven, as a trophy of redeeming grace.

Turn for a moment more to earth, and look at the temporal achievements of the ministry. What hath God wrought by preaching? The Roman empire was Christianized by preaching—the preaching of Paul and his noble companions. And though the "weapons of their warfare were not carnal, yet they were mighty through God, to the pulling down of strongholds." There sat Paganism at the capital, enthroned above the heads of kings and emperors—clad in all her dazzling splendor—with her magnificent temples—her gorgeous train of priests—her holy vestal virgins—her learned interpreters of the sibylline oracles—her gladiatorial shows—her vast amphitheatres, some of which could contain tens of thousands of spectators. But Paul preached, and institutions venerable by ages tottered and fell. The glorious Reformation was chiefly brought about by *preaching*—the preaching of Luther. The Republic of Geneva, after which our own Republic was fashioned, was produced by *preaching*, the preaching of Calvin. The sturdy national character of Scotland was formed chiefly by the preaching of men like John Knox, of whom at his grave it was said, "There lies one who never feared the face of men." The present quiet of every New England village was laid far back in the preaching of the Stoddards, and the Mathers, and the Edwardses. The present national existence of the Sandwich Islands, whose people forty years ago were wild cannibals, is the fruit of the preaching of American missionaries. The foundations of the American Union were laid in the labors and toils of such men as George Fox, the Quaker, and John Wesley, the Methodist, and George Whitfield, the Calvinist, who traveled and preached from Massachusetts to Georgia, and aided the people to form religious and ecclesiastical affinities, before the cry to arms rung out from old Faneuil Hall. Civil liberty, in the days of our fathers, was perched upon the standard of the cross, and will always visit every land where that standard is unfurled. And the conversion of the nations to God, and the final and universal triumphs of the Gospel, will be effected mainly by the same heaven-ordained and heaven-owned method. For the Lord shall give the word; great shall be the army of the publishers. "For an angel shall be seen, flying through the clouds of heaven, having the everlasting Gospel to preach to every nation." And as that blessed Gospel shall begin to walk abroad on its last triumph, thrones shall tremble, oracles shall grow dumb, and the brows of tyrants shall turn white as ashes. Then cities and palaces shall fling wide their gates at her advancing tread, and the great mass of suffering, sinful men shall bow their adoring heads as her sweet voice shall fall upon their ear.

1. In view of all that has been said, it is expedient that there should be a much more exalted appreciation of the ministerial office. It should be magnified above all other callings. Is he deemed great who founds empires, gains victories, amasses wealth, or glitters in stars and coronets—whose praises live in history, and whose name is engraven on marble? How much more honorable, and how much more deserving of gratitude, should they be deemed who ameliorate the hearts of men, subdue passions, found churches, form public morals, and produce effects on character and conduct that shall last forever.

2. We also see, from this subject, the propriety of setting apart a distinct class of men to the ministerial work. If the ministry be of divine appointment, honored of God, magnified of Paul, filled by Christ, surely not every one is competent to enter it, and none should enter upon it, but he that is "called of God, as was Aaron"—called by the Church, called by his own brethren, called by the Spirit, called by his own heart, glowing with love for souls, and appropriating the words of the Apostle, "for necessity is laid upon me, yea, woe is me if I preach not the Gospel." And when such a one has assumed the ministry, he should never desert it. He should wear out in it, and become every day more and more a centre of influence, and a saver of life unto life to immortal souls. Alas for those who do not thus magnify their office. Woe to those who degrade the ministry—detract from its heavenly dignity by perverting it to secular purposes, and "steal the livery of the court of heaven to serve the devil in." Among such we include sectarian preachers, poetical preachers, sensational preachers, political preachers, fanatical preachers.

3. Contemplate the elevated position of our Church in its high appreciation of the dignity and sacredness of the office, in permitting none to enter it but men of piety and learning, that the ark of the Lord be not carried by inefficient or unholy hands. Hence the honorable distinction of our Zion in her zeal in educating the young, in founding schools and colleges, and furnishing the world with a learned ministry.

4. You here learn the duty of the people to provide for the temporal wants of the ministry. If we minister to you in spiritual things, is it not a small matter that you should contribute to us of your temporal things? Is not the laborer worthy of his hire? Should not they who serve at the altar, live of the altar? And is not that church most criminally remiss in her duty to herself and her head, which expects of her ministry constant services and elevated mental toil, but which extends to them a scanty and niggard support, expecting men to be given to hospitality and devoted to study, as well as punctual in meeting their pecuniary obligations, but whose worldly maintenance is inadequate or paid with reluctance.

5. The views which we have advanced respecting the ministry, so far from begetting in the mind feelings of vain glory, are calulated to instill the deepest humility. When we recount our arduous duties, our severe trials, and our fearful responsibilities, we would cry out with the Apostle: "Who is sufficient for these things?" Oh, brethren, "we are with you in weakness, and in fear, and in much trembling." And we would appeal to you in the language of the same Apostle, "Brethren, pray for us." Nothing will so much relieve us, nothing will so much encourage us, as your fervent prayers. For a prayerless people will always have a desponding ministry; while, on the other hand, the performance of this

duty will lead to the performance of every other. They who pray for their pastor will necessarily love him; they will contribute to his worldly support; they will be careful of his reputation; they will punctually wait on his ministry; they will receive with meekness the word of God from his lips, will grow up with him as heirs of the grace of life, and finally enter with him into the same eternal joy.

HISTORY

OF THE

PRESBYTERIAN CHURCH,

HOUSTON, TEXAS.

THIS church was organized on the 31st of March, 1839, in the Senate Chamber of the Congress of the Republic of Texas, by Rev. William Y. Allen, after a sermon preached by him from Psalm cxxii., verse 6: "Pray for the peace of Jerusalem, they shall prosper that love thee."

The following preamble and resolutions were adopted as the basis of organization, viz.:

"For the purpose of promoting Divine worship, and our mutual edification in the knowledge and practice of piety, we, whose names are hereunto subscribed, do agree to associate ourselves together as a Presbyterian Church upon the following principles, viz.:

"1st. We believe the Scriptures of the Old and New Testaments to be the Word of God, the only infallible rule of faith and practice.

"2d. We sincerely adopt the Confession of Faith of the Presbyterian Church in the United States of America as containing the system of doctrine taught in the Holy Scriptures.

"3d. We adopt the form of Government and Directory for worship as laid down in the Constitution of the Presbyterian Church in the United States of America."

To the above agreement the following names were appended:

A. B. Shelby, Marian Shelby,
J. Wilson Copes, James Bailey,
James Burke, Sarah Woodward,
Isabella R. Parker, Jennett Smith,
Edwin Belden, Harris G. Avery,
Sophia B. Hodge.

The organization was completed by the election of James Burke to the office of Ruling Elder.

On the 14th of April, 1839, the sacrament of the Lord's Supper was administered to twenty-five communicants. This was the first celebration of this sacrament in Houston, most probably the first in Texas.

After organizing the church, Rev. W. Y. Allen continued to minister to it until the spring of 1842, when he resigned and returned to Kentucky, and was succeeded by

REV. J. M. ATKINSON,

then on a visit to Texas. He received a unanimous call to become pastor of the church. Finding his health unfitted him for the labors of the office, he declined the call, and left the State early in 1843, having served the church about one year.

In the spring of 1843, application was made to the Board of Foreign Missions of the Presbyterian Church, in the United States, which commissioned the Rev. J. W. Miller as a missionary to this field.

REV. J. W. MILLER

arrived December, 1844, and entered on the discharge of his duties. He received a unanimous call to the pastorate, and was installed November 21, 1847. His health failing, he resigned the charge in January, 1850, having been five years over the congregation, during which time seventy members were admitted to the church.

REV. L. S. GIBSON,

being in the city, received a unanimous call from the church and congregation. His health failed under two severe bilious attacks, in 1850 and 1851, which caused him to cease preaching. He died in Philadelphia, in

May, 1853, while in attendance on the General Assembly, as commissioner from the presbytery of Brazos.

On December 31, 1851, an invitation to supply the pulpit for one year, was made to

REV. ALEX. FAIRBAIRN.

In 1853, he received a call for his services as pastor, and was installed in February of that year. He resigned his charge in December, 1854, and moved to Huntsville.

REV. JEROME TWICHELL

was installed as pastor of the church in April, 1855, and was lost on the "Nautilus," in the Gulf, during the storm of August 10, 1856.

REV. R. H. BYERS

was called on June 20, 1857, and entered on his ministration in the following September.

In November, 1859, he accepted the financial agency of Austin College, by which the pulpit again became vacant. He was succeeded by

REV. THOS. CASTLETON,

called in April, 1860, and installed April, 1861; he filled the pulpit during the greater part of the war.

On October 25, 1862, the church, a frame building, fronting on Main-street, was destroyed by fire. Under the exertions of Mr. Castleton, plans were speedily matured to replace it by a brick structure, which he was not permitted to see completed. In October, 1864, his relations with the church were dissolved by presbytery. In 1865—with his wife—he embarked on the "Shibboleth" for New York, and is supposed to have been lost at sea, as that vessel was not heard of any more after leaving Galveston.

After the fire, worship was conducted in the Court House, until it was taken for barracks, when Turner's Hall was obtained by

REV. J. R. HUTCHISON, D. D.,

who preached every Sabbath morning until June, 1865, when the hall had to be given up.

The *New Building* was *dedicated* on Sabbath, July 7, 1867, by Rev. R. H. Byers, D. D., assisted by Rev. S. A. King and Mr. Moore. On April 1, 1868,

REV. WM. SOMERVILLE

was invited to supply the pulpit one year, when the regular services of the church, after a long interruption, were resumed. He was installed pastor of the church in May, 1869, and resigned in October, 1870. On September, 1871,

REV. JNO. J. READ,

a licentiate of the presbytery of Mississippi, received the unanimous call of the church and congregation to become pastor thereof, having accepted the same, he was dismissed to the care of the presbytery of Brazos.

After having sustained a satisfactory examination, the presbytery proceeded on Sabbath, December 10, to ordain him to the full work of the Gospel ministry, the Moderator, Rev. R. F. Bunting, D.D., presiding. The Rev. J. R. Hutchison, D.D., was appointed to preach the Ordination Sermon; Rev. J. W. Miller, D. D., to deliver a charge to the congregation, and Rev. R. F. Bunting, D. D., a charge to the pastor.

THE SABBATH.

Preached at Hempstead, Texas, October, 1869.

"*Remember the Sabbath day to keep it holy.*"—Exodus 20 : 8. The observance of the Sabbath is essential to the spread of Christianity, and to its transmission from one age to another. The Sabbath is the centre of the system, the keystone of the arch. Without it, the Gospel would have no opportunity of exerting its benign influences upon the masses, of giving forth, in public assemblies, its loud and solemn utterances of warning and instruction. For how could mankind retain a knowledge of the great doctrines of the Cross, unless they were plainly and publicly taught them? And how could they be publicly taught them, unless there were a specific day on which, by common consent, they might assemble for the purpose?

The necessity and importance, therefore, of the Sabbath, as a day of religious instruction and meditation, the honor which it confers on God, the peace and quiet which it brings to man, the rest it imparts to the body, the solemn pause it secures to all the secularities of life —these, with other most weighty considerations, combine in enforcing the command of the Decalogue, "Remember the Sabbath day, to keep it holy."

It has, however, been contended by some that the Sabbath day is a Jewish institution, and being merely national and ceremonial in its character, is not of perpetual and universal obligation. But can it not be shown that the Sabbath was instituted long before the Jewish nation existed, and although incorporated into the civil and ecclesiastical polity of that people, it never exclusively belonged to them, but is binding, in all its force, upon the people of every country and every age?

Our first argument is drawn from its great antiquity. The Sabbath was instituted two thousand years before the Jewish nation existed. It is as old as the creation. It was given by God to the first man, Adam. It is then binding on us; because Adam was a public character, and acted in a public capacity. Adam was not merely our great progenitor; he was also our federal head and representative. Adam negotiated with the court of heaven, not only for himself, but for all his posterity. This is one of the plainest doctrines of the Bible. Consequently, according to the laws of imputation and representation, all Adam's acts become our acts, all Adam's institutions become our institutions. If, then, the institution of the Sabbath was observed by Adam, it must be observed by us, for the same reason that we observe the institution of marriage.

Where, then, is the evidence that the Sabbath was known to our great representative? It is found in the book of Genesis, second chapter, second and third verses: "On the seventh day God ended His work which He had made, and He rested on the seventh day from all His work which He had made. And God blessed the seventh day and sanctified it, because that on it He had rested from all His work which God created and made." Adam was created on the sixth day; the next day was the sacred day of rest. Hence the first rising sun which Adam ever saw, ushered in the hallowed rest of the new-born Sabbath.

But we have other evidence that the Sabbath is as old as the creation. We find traces of its existence and partial observance in the history of every nation of antiquity, both Jewish and heathen. Begin with the history of the Jews in the wilderness, as they were journeying from Egypt to Palestine, and before they reached Mount Sinai. Observe how regularly they abstained from the gathering of manna, at the close of every sixth day, in order that they might rest on the seventh. Mark how familiarly Moses refers to the Sabbath in the giving of the ten commandments. He there takes for granted that the Jews knew of the Sabbath before the giving of the law on Sinai. For he says, "*Remember* the Sabbath," implying that it had been previously known.

Now go further back into the history of the Jews, and you will still find proofs of the existence of the Sabbath. Examine the history of Job, forty years previous to the giving of the law, and you will find familiar mention of the Sabbath. Go two hundred and fifty years further back, to the time of Jacob, and you will observe that he observed the Sabbath. Go one hundred and fifty years further back, to the time of Abraham, and you will find that he knew the Sabbath. Then go back four hundred and fifty years further, to the time of Noah, and you will perceive that he also observed the Sabbath. In this day, the Sabbath can be traced back to Adam.

Now turn from the history of the Jews to the history of early heathen nations, and go back until all history is lost in fable or is merged in the Mosaic narrative. The Sabbath is mentioned by Homer, the father of Greek poetry. He says, "The seventh day is the day on which all things were finished." It is referred to by Lineus, another early Grecian writer, who says, "The seventh day is an auspicious day, for it is the birthday of all things." It is mentioned by Philo, an early

Egyptian writer. He asserts that "the Sabbath is a festival, not peculiar to any one country, but is common to all the world." Josephus, the Jewish historian, tells us that in his day "there was no city, either of Greeks or barbarians, where the obligation of the Sabbath was not known." And the learned Grotius declares "that the memory of the creation being performed in the seven days, was preserved not only among the Greeks and Italians, but also among the Celts and Indians, all of whom divided their time into weeks." Thus we find traces of the Sabbath among all the nations of antiquity.

And now the important question presents itself: How did those early heathen nations acquire their knowledge of the Sabbath? Whence could have arisen this universal practice of dividing time into weeks, and of showing such marked deference to the seventh day? How happened it that people inhabiting different countries, speaking different languages, and adhering to different religions, all agree in this one practice? Would their notions respecting astronomy have led them to such a division of time? No; their astronomical views would have led them to divide their time into months and days and years, but would never have suggested to them a division of time into weeks. Weeks are unnatural divisions of time, suggested by no revolutions of the heavenly bodies. Nor did the ancient heathen derive their knowledge of weeks from the Jews. For many of these nations existed before the Jews were embodied into a nation. Some of them never heard of the Jews, and some entertained for Jewish customs a very strong abhorrence.

The only method, then, of accounting for the early and universal practice of dividing time into weeks, is that it was communicated by God to Adam in Paradise, as was the rite of marriage, handed down by tradition among the antediluvian patriarchs, then scattered, after the flood, among all the nations of the earth.

We base the perpetual obligation of the Sabbath, not merely upon its institution in Paradise, its recognition among all the nations of antiquity, and its incorporation into the Jewish economy, but mainly on the fact of its constituting a prominent part of the ten commandments. Hence, all who admit the universal and perpetual obligation of the Decalogue, must admit the equally binding nature of the Sabbath.

For if the Sabbath was merely ceremonial, serving a temporary purpose, and then passing away, like other temporary rites of the old dispensation, why should it occupy such a prominent place in that code of laws designed by God to be binding on the whole human race? Why is it found there at all? Why select it from the number of the merely temporary ordinances of the Mosaic economy, and place it so conspicuously in the very centre of that eternal compendium of moral duties, given for the government of the whole world? The fact of its being found where it is decides the question. And there is something in the peculiar position which this command occupies in the Decalogue, and the language in which it is couched, which renders it the most remarkable precept of the entire ten. It is the *longest* commandment. It is the most minute and specific in its language, carefully enumerating a large number of particulars. It is located in the very *heart* of the code, between the two tables of the law—the first embracing our duties to God, the second our duties to man. And because this precept partakes of the nature of both tables, and enjoins duties to both God and man, it is placed *between* both. It is the *golden clasp* which binds the two tables together; and whoever would take it away, breaks the clasp and mars the whole. For he robs God of his worship and man of his rest. The fact, then, of the law of the Sabbath being found in the Decalogue, settles the question under discussion. And mankind have no more right to violate or ignore its requirements, than they have to set aside the law respecting idolatry, or murder, or theft, or filial insubordination, or conjugal infidelity.

Another weighty argument for the obligation of the Sabbath, is derived from considering the great *design* for which it was originally instituted. What was that design? It was of the most beneficial nature. It was that man might have time to rest his body, improve his mind, and purify his heart; that he might have sufficient respite from physical toil—sufficient leisure to worship God and prepare for eternity. Now, are not these uses of the Sabbath just as important now as they ever were, and, therefore, is not the observance of the Sabbath just as necessary? Does not man require just as much time to rest his body, to improve his mind, to purify his heart, to serve his God, and to prepare for eternity, as he did in the juvenile ages? It is the testimony of anatomists, that the constitutions of both man and beast absolutely require one-seventh portion of time for rest and relaxation, or else they will soon wear out. Behold, then, the wonderful adaptation of this part of the moral government of God, for the physical constitution of man. And if it was necessary that the ancient patriarchs and the other early inhabitants of the world, should have one-seventh portion of their time for rest and relaxation, is it not far more important that we should have the same rest? The bodies of men and beasts now are not half so vigorous as they were in those early ages, and require more rest and more leisure. And the laborious employments of men now are far greater than they were then. For in those primeval days of simplicity, men had little else to do than to attend to their peaceful flocks, shoot the passing game, and drink the crystal stream. And still they needed a day of rest. How much more do *we* need it. Now, arguing from the design for which the Sabbath day was originally instituted, we may safely argue the necessity of its continuation and perpetuity. Does the cause for which it was originally given exist still? then should not the day exist likewise? So long as man's physical nature remains what it is; so long as the soul retains its importance; so long as man shall sweat and toil both in body and mind the larger portion of his time, just so long does he need the merciful provision of the Sabbath. If Adam in Paradise required the sacred day of rest, much more do his sinful descendants need it. Not, then, as punishment, but as a merciful condescension to our infirmities, has God said, "Remember the Sabbath-day, to keep it holy."

The obligation to sanctify the Sabbath, in addition to what has been set forth in our former issues, receives still greater force by contemplating the great *blessings* and *advantages* resulting from its observance, and the sad results flowing from its desecration. In enumerating these blessings both to soul and body, both to man as an individual and as a member of the social compact, both as a dweller on earth and as a candidate for heaven, where shall we begin, and where end?

By keeping the Sabbath, those who are compelled to toil during the week are permitted to rest and recruit their exhausted energies. Men of business and speculation are permitted to pause in their career of bargaining and sales, have time to reflect calmly and dispassionately, and are thus often held back from sudden bankruptcy or a too great love of money. Those also whose incessant occupations during the week prevent them from having access to books find time to read and improve their minds. Attention can be given to dress and cleanliness, and to the polite civilities of friends. People of all classes can assemble together in the house of God. The high and the low, the rich and the poor, meet together upon a perfect equality. They are taught to feel that they have a common God and a common Saviour; a common origin—a common end. They are also instructed in these things in the best possible manner. For there is something in the presence of a crowd, in the power of sympathy, and in the thrilling tones of the human voice, which renders the public preaching of the gospel, and the songs and prayers of the sanctuary, the most effective means of impressing divine truth upon the hearts of men. They who are unable to read and improve themselves at home, can listen to the reading and reasoning of another. Impressions are thus made which are deep and lasting. A thousand conflicting passions are harmonized. The affections are weaned from earth and soar towards heaven. The pious are edified; the ignorant are instructed; the wicked are warned; the wavering are confirmed. A love for morality and order is diffused from heart to heart, and from family to family. The community is improved; intelligence is diffused; crimes are diminished. A moral sentiment is spread all around, which forms a more effectual preservation of the liberties of the country than pikes and armies. Oh! in view of such blessings, who ought not to love the Sabbath? What patriot, what Christian, what lover of his own family, what friend of the poor, should not sanctify the Sabbath?

But reverse this pleasing picture and view the result. Abolish the Sabbath, and you take away every one of the blessings we have enumerated, and you substitute a corresponding curse. Abolish the Sabbath, and you give the laboring class no stated time to rest, and the commercial class no regular period to pause in their career of worldliness. Abolish the Sabbath, and you place in its stead no other effectual method of instructing the ignorant, of restraining the vicious, or of improving the manners of the masses without injuring their morals. In a word, take away the Sabbath, and you give us no other method of diffusing the blessings of Christianity. And if Christianity be not diffused, virtue, morality, and liberty must soon bid farewell to the land. Nothing but the power of the Gospel can purify and save this nation. Nothing but this can preserve us from the effects of infidelity, of intemperance, of party-strife, and national pride. Our general intelligence, our growing wealth, our ardent patriotism, and our invincible courage cannot, of themselves, preserve us. They did not preserve Greece, or Rome, or France. Hence nothing but the Sabbath, as a means of inculcating our holy religion, can preserve the fair temple of American liberty. Nothing but a phalanx of holy hearts clustering thick around the Sabbath, can preserve us from going down to the gloomy grave of nations.

We have had an instance in modern times, of a whole nation deliberately abolishing the Sabbath, and what was the result? No sooner had France blotted out this moral sun from her heavens, than the mighty God whose being she denied, and whose worship she ignored, stood aloof and gave her up; and a scene of proscription and assassination and crime ensued, unparalleled in the annals of the civilized world. Every moral and domestic tie was ruthlessly torn asunder. A brother's hand was deeply imbrued in a brother's blood. The tears of the lisping babe, the shrieks of the agonized mother, and the frantic cries of hoary and decrepit age, mingled with the demoniac shouts of an infuriated soldiery, dragging their victims to the guillotine. Yea, says one, it seemed as if the nation's knell had tolled, and the whole world was summoned to the funeral. In the city of Paris, there were in 1803 eight hundred and seven suicides and murders. Among the criminals executed, there were seven fathers who had poisoned their children, ten husbands who had murdered their wives, six wives who had poisoned their husbands—and fifteen children who had destroyed their parents! Do then the Infidels of this land desire to have the scenes of revolutionary France re-enacted, let them abolish the Sabbath, and forthwith, from the vasty deep will come up the demons of blood. The Sabbath is the "cord by which God holds up the nation from the gulf that rolls beneath it." While, then, one strand of this cord after another is cut, what can prevent, when the last cord is severed, this mighty nation, like the massive rock on the mountain's cliff, from thundering down to ruin. Give up the Sabbath—blot out that orb of day—suspend its blessed attractions—and the reign of chaos and old night will return. The waves of our unquiet sea will roll and dash, shipwrecking the hopes of patriots and the world. The elements around us may remain, and our gigantic mountains and rivers; our miserable descendants may multiply and rot in moral darkness and putrefaction. But the American character and the American nation will go down into the same grave that entombs the Sabbath—and our epitaph will be, "Here ended the nation that despised the laws of heaven, and gloried in their wisdom, wealth, and power."

Be entreated then, to "Remember the Sabbath-day to keep it holy." This is the day the Lord hath made. He calls the hours his own. Remember it, for it comes to rest the weary laborer, to calm the fevered brow of the anxious merchant. Remember it, for it is the type of heaven—of that rest which remaineth for the people of God. Remember it, for God wrote it with his own finger upon tables of stone, and proclaimed it, amid thunderings and lightning and earthquakes, from the summit of Mount Sinai. Remember it, because of the awful judgments inflicted on those nations and individuals who have violated it—on rebellious Israel, on Infidel France, when God thinned their families, wasted their treasures, and drenched their cities in blood. Remember it, because of the many terrible calamities which have come under your own observation in consequence of its violation—the carriage accident—the boat disaster—the faithless gun—the gay party of pleasure, which went out on the morning of God's holy day, but who never returned, or else were brought home mere mangled corpses, monuments of the wrath of heaven.

We never, in the whole course of our recollection, met with a Christian friend who bore upon his character any evidence of the spirit's renovation, who did not keep holy the Sabbath. "We appeal to the memory of all the worthies who are now lying in their graves; we appeal to every one who reads these lines, and who carries in his bosom a recollection of a father's worth and a mother's piety, if, on the coming round of the seventh day, an air of peculiar sacredness did not spread itself over the mansion where he drew his first breath, and was taught to lisp his infant hymn, and breathe his infant prayer. The Sabbath is still dear to him. He loves the quietness of the hallowed morn. He loves the church bell sound, which summons him to the house of prayer. He loves to join the chorus of devotion, and sit and listen to the voice of persuasion, which is lifted up in the hearing of the great congregation."

A CHRISTMAS STORY.

Preached at Baton Rouge, November 25, 1831.

"*Behold, I bring you good tidings of great joy, which shall be to all people.*"—Luke 2:10. The silence of midnight reigns over Judea. The inhabitants of the city of Bethlehem are reposing in peaceful slumber, all save a few humble herdsmen upon a neighboring field. The notes of a shepherd's pipe float across the moonlit plain. Suddenly those notes are hushed; for music of a loftier strain—music such as is set and sung in heaven—comes along the breeze. A seraph's wing rustles in the sky, a seraph's dazzling form comes down, a seraph's voice proclaims the embassy, "Behold, I bring you good tidings of great joy, which shall be to all people. For unto you is born this day, in the city of David, a Saviour, which is Christ the Lord. And suddenly there was with the angel a multitude of the heavenly host, praising God, and saying, Glory to God in the highest, and on earth peace, good will toward men."

Oh, what emotions of rapture must have thrilled through those shepherds' hearts, as this announcement fell from the angel's lips! "The predicted Messiah, the long-expected deliverer of the world, has He at last come? That glorious Personage, the theme of many a poet's song, the burden of many a prophet's rapture, has He at last actually appeared? And now no more shall the nations mourn; no longer shall their ardent expectations be disappointed. The darkness of superstition will now roll away; the types will all be fulfilled; the spirituality of a once sublime system of worship will be restored; the blind shall see, the deaf hear, the lame man shall leap as an hart, and the tongue of the dumb sing; for the Lord whom we have long sought has come to his temple. Let us haste to the city, and worship the heavenly stranger."

Was this announcement of the incarnation an event of intense interest to the Jew, it is equally so to the Gentile. For hear its language: "Behold, I bring you good tidings of great joy, which shall be to all people." And all people have had reason so to view it. The assumption of human nature by the Son of God was the commencement of that chain of glorious events which received their consummation on Calvary, constituting a scheme of redemption for sinners of every age and nation, forming a river of free grace, which has rolled and widened, and watered the earth; upon whose sacred brink *we* are permitted to stand and drink and never die. Yea, must not the historian, in tracing all the improvements of modern society to their true cause, go directly back to him who was born in a manger in Bethlehem, and expired as a malefactor on the Cross? For what else but his benign religion—the combined product of his incarnation, his example, his teachings, and his death—has changed the aspect of our world; communicating its kindly influences to every public and private department of life; working itself into the framework of civil states; giving a tinge to the complexion of governments, to the temper and administration of laws; restraining the spirit of princes and the madness of the people; softening the rigor of despotism; blunting the edge of the sword, and spreading a vail of mercy over the horrors of modern warfare? Its kindly influences have descended into families, improved every domestic endearment, given tenderness to the parent, humanity to the master, respect to superiors, to inferiors ease. And what is its influence on our prospects of a life to come? It is all our dependence and all our hope. When the soul is burdened under a sense of guilt, how readily it reverts to those awful scenes which occurred eighteen hundred years ago. There, while dwelling by a retrospective faith upon Bethlehem and Gethsemane and the Cross, the hard heart is softened into penitence and love. There death itself has lost its sting, and the soul, with a holy magnanimity, has borne up under the terrors of dissolution, and has sung old Simeon's song, "Lord, now lettest thou thy servant depart in peace, for mine eyes have seen thy salvation."

Behold, then, we bring you good tidings of great joy, which shall be to all people. All people are benefited by his birth, all people are instructed by his life, all people are saved, if saved at all, by his death. The time of the advent was one of great joy.

1. Christ became incarnate at a period in which the whole civilized world were *expecting* him. History asserts that not merely were the Jews at that time confidently looking for the promised Messiah, but also that a profound impression was pervading all civilized nations, that a glorious personal personage was about to arise to reform and bless the whole earth. Hence, as if by a common impulse, the nations had laid aside their bloody conflicts, and were reposing in unwonted harmony. Wars had ceased. The temple of Janus at Rome was closed. The blessings of peace were enjoyed throughout the vast Roman empire. The wise men of Greece and Rome and Persia, impelled either from a secret impulse from heaven, or else from the influence of a wide-spread tradition, were all casting their anxious gaze to the land of Judea, as the place from which would

speedily issue the world's great deliverer. And thus we read, that when Jesus was born in Bethlehem in Judea, in the days of Herod the king, there came wise men from the East to Jerusalem, saying, "Where is he that is born King of the Jews? For we have seen his star in the East, and are come to worship him." And guided by that mysterious star, they came to the place where the sleeping infant lay, and bowing down before him, they gave him their gold, their frankincense, and their myrrh.

2. The incarnation of Christ occurred at a time his presence was *most needed.* It is a historical fact, no less strange than true, that the period of the advent was a period of unprecedented moral darkness. The repose of the nations was the slumber of spiritual death. Notwithstanding Jerusalem had her temple, Greece her academic groves, and Rome her senate and her forum, and all three had their priests, their poets, and their orators, yet still a gloomy night of ignorance, superstition, and vice, brooded over the earth. The Jewish Church had utterly lost her spirituality, and was reposing complacently on mere external ceremonies. The Pharisee, on the one hand, placed all religion in mere external morality. The Sadducee, on the other hand, destroyed all religion by denying the immortality of the soul. Was such the condition of the Jews, what was the state of the Gentiles? Darker still. The nations had sunk into the most abject ignorance on moral topics, and were calling on their wise men for light and knowledge, but all in vain. The speculations of human reason, the refinements of human philosophy, all the elegant accomplishments of the Augustan age, had utterly failed in elevating the morals and restraining the vices of men. Yea, their gods were hideous monsters, debauchery and crime. There was not a single

vice, in the dark catalogue of human enormities, which was not shamelessly perpetrated under the sanction of some one of those innumerable gods and goddesses before whose shrines the nations bowed. "The world by wisdom knew not God." Then it was clearly demonstrated that no attainments of poetry, eloquence, or science, however great, can supersede the necessity of divine revelation; that a man may be affluent in all the riches of learning, and glittering in all the attractions of wit, and still need a teacher from heaven, a divine physician to heal his moral maladies, a supernatural light from the skies to dispel the darkness of his soul. Hence the declaration of a heathen writer of that day, that unless the gods sent down to earth a special messenger, the nations must wax worse and worse. Now, in view of these facts, I ask you, when was such a being as Jesus Christ more needed? When was such a deliverer more longed for? And what was calculated to give more joy to the earth than the announcement of his incarnation?

3. The period of the incarnation was the best possible period for the propagation of a new religion. Not merely did the world expect a Saviour—not merely did the debased state of the world absolutely need his presence—but the condition of the nations at that time presented peculiar facilities for the spread of a new faith. The fullness of the time had come. There was the Greek language—the language of Christ and his apostles—the language of poetry and passion, spoken throughout the civilized world—standing ready to serve as a most happy vehicle for the spread of a new religion. Never had there been a period in which there was greater intercourse between the various nations of the earth. All the large cities were filled with strangers. Merchants and philosophers were continually traveling from

city to city, in search of wealth and knowledge. Hence we read that when Peter stood up on the day of Pentecost and preached his first sermon, he was heard by the representatives of seventeen different nations—"Parthians, and Medes, and Elamites, and the dwellers in Mesopotamia, and in Judea, and Cappadocia, in Pontus, and Asia, Phrygia, and Pamphylia, in Egypt, and in the parts of Libya about Cyrene, and strangers of Rome, Jews and proselytes, Cretes and Arabians, we do hear them speak in our tongues the wonderful works of God. And they were all amazed, and were in doubt, saying one to another, What meaneth this?" And returning to their distant homes, they spread the wondrous story. Oh what an auspicious era for the coming of our Lord!

4. The time of the advent was the time accurately foretold by the prophets of the old dispensation. The seventy weeks of Daniel were now drawing to a close. The types and ceremonies—the slaughtering of sheep and of goats—all the solemn pomp of the Jewish worship, were pointing in a manner not to be misunderstood, to the speedy coming of the Lamb of God, who, by the sacrifice of himself upon the Cross, would take away the sins of the world. There are nearly two hundred prophecies in the Old Testament Scriptures, which clearly indicated the approaching advent. One prophet had predicted the circumstances of his birth—another, the tribe from which he would spring—a third, the very month of his incarnation. Had he not then appeared at the specified time and place, the credit of the Old Testament as a divine Revelation would have been forever destroyed. But "behold we bring you good tidings of great joy;" for unto you was born in the city of David, a Saviour. By being so born, he has fulfilled the prophecies, abolished the sacrifices, broken down the middle wall of partition between Jew and Gentile, and

has purchased everlasting salvation for men of every age, and tribe, and people. "Glory be to God in the highest, on earth peace, good will to men." In Christ there is neither Jew nor Greek, Barbarian, Scythian, bond or free—but all are one, one Lord, one faith, one baptism, one church, and one heaven.

5. We come now to the most important consideration which made the incarnation of Jesus a source of "great joy to all people." "Jesus was born in Bethlehem of Judea," in order that he might die upon the cross for the redemption of a lost world. Or, as St. Paul expresses it, "When the fullness of the time was come, God so loved the world, that he gave his only begotten Son, that whosoever believeth on him might not perish, but have everlasting life." No wonder that a multitude of the heavenly host came down and sung glory to God in the highest, and on earth, peace, good will to men. And why all this? Why the awful mystery of the incarnation? Why must the second person in the Godhead be wrapt in a veil of mortal flesh? Why born of a woman and cradled in a manger?

Man is placed under the moral government of God. No moral government can exist without law. No law has any force without penalty. Penalties are useless, unless they are executed. Must God reward the righteous, when they obey? Then, for the same reason, he is bound to punish the wicked when they transgress. Could the honor of his law, could the stability of his throne, could the well-being of the universe for one moment be maintained, were he to permit the guilty to escape? Who then have incurred the penalty? Man. Who can remove the penalty? Christ. "Christ hath redeemed us from the curse of the law, having been made a curse for us." He bore the load. He endured the penalty. He paid down the ransom. He released the captive. He redeemed the slave. His wounds are our healing—his groans, our songs—his death, our life—his crown of thorns, our crown of glory. But could not Christ achieve this great work, without becoming incarnate? No. Human nature had sinned. Hence, human nature must suffer. For, "without shedding of blood, there is no remission." Blood, then, must first be possessed, before blood could be shed. Hence the absolute necessity, that the Redeemer should become *man*—man to set us an example, man to enable him to sympathize with humanity, man to suffer death in the room of the guilty. Equally essential was it, that He should be *God;* otherwise, his sufferings and death, however agonizing, could have had nothing meritorious, no more than the death of the martyrs. Christ must needs be man, to qualify him to suffer; he must needs be God, to impart to his sufferings infinite merit. And by virtue of his being both God and man, he of all beings in heaven and earth, is qualified to be the Redeemer of the world. By the union of the two natures, the blood of Calvary becomes efficacious, and mercy flows down to a lost race. "Behold the man! How glorious He."

Are you guilty? We bring you good tidings; Christ hath delivered us from the curse of the law. Are you tempted? Here are good tidings. "He is able to succor them that are tempted."

Are you bowed down under the troubles of life? Hear him saying, "Come unto me all ye that labor and are heavy laden."

Are ye poor? He is the poor man's friend. Are you afraid to die? He hath abolished death, and become the conqueror of the king of terrors. Finally, to one and to all, we bring good news. In the effects of his wonderful incarnation, you are all interested—of the fruits of his death, you are all invited to partake. Because he became man, you may become kings and priests unto God. You may, however, neglect the offer—refuse the message—turn a deaf ear to tidings that made all heaven glad; the time will come when this strange indifference will be over. "Pleasure will fold her wing, and friend and lover shall to the embraces of the worm have gone." The moment you enter eternity, how changed the scene. The love of Christ, the infinite felicity of being saved, the unspeakable misery of being lost, will occupy the vast capacities of the immortal soul.

THE HOPE OF THE NATION.

Preached in Houston, Dec. 16, 1864, by request of President Davis.

"*For the nation and kingdom that will not serve thee shall perish; yea, those nations shall be utterly wasted.*"—Isaiah 60 : 12. Nations exist only in this life. Hence, they receive all their rewards and all their punishments here. And they are rewarded or punished in proportion to the degree in which they obey or transgress the laws of Heaven. It is a truth susceptible of the clearest moral demonstration that righteousness exalteth a nation as well as an individual, and that "Godliness is profitable for all things, having the promise of the life that now is, and that which is to come." If the Gospel were permitted to exert its proper influence upon the kingdoms of the world, the highest degree of temporal happiness and prosperity would be the sure result. Civil liberty is perched upon the standard of the Cross, and will visit every land where that standard is unfurled. In the religion of the Bible we have an unfailing antidote against all those moral maladies which in past ages have brought ruin on nations. The Gospel proposes to change the hearts of men—to soften their tempers—to impart a holy direction to the governing purposes of the soul—thus leading men to be moral and virtuous from *principle;* not from constraint, but from choice—not from the dread of temporal punishments, but from a cheerful preference. The Gospel is opposed to ambition, the bane of empires. It forbids revenge, the usual cause of national conflicts. It condemns avarice, the prolific parent of oppression, dishonesty, and fraud. It denounces idleness, and declares that "if a man will not work, neither shall he eat." It imposes a solemn restriction on the animal appetites, "teaching us that, denying ungodliness and worldly lusts, we should live soberly, righteously, and godly in this present world," thus cutting off ten thousand avenues to misery, violence, and blood. The Gospel inculcates the fear of an invisible but omnipotent Jehovah, and thus leads men to be virtuous in secret—to reverence the obligation of oaths, upon the observance of which property, reputation, and life so frequently depend. It likewise teaches us to love our country—to defend our rights—to obey magistrates—to pity and help the poor. It elevates the female sex, and gives woman her proper rank in the social state. It proclaims the original equality of the human race, and thus frowns upon the arrogant claims of kings—the divine right of the few to rule the many, of the strong to oppress the weak.

Are such some of the pure and elevating principles of our holy religion, all must at once perceive that their belief and practice would exalt the nations of the earth, and make them great, glorious, and free. And therefore, must not every community in which these principles are unknown be poor and abject—a prey to misrule and faction, and, in its gradual but sure decline, soon exhibit a melancholy illustration of the truth of the text, that "the nation and kingdom that will not serve God shall perish; yea those nations shall be utterly wasted?"

But if it be true that the belief and practice of the precepts of the Gospel can alone make nations great, the remark applies with most peculiar force to a country like ours. Here the people govern themselves. All authority and all power emanates from them. Hence if the people be not enlightened and virtuous, our experiment of self-government must assuredly fail. If the fountain be impure, the streams will be polluted, and will form a river of death, which will desolate and curse our fair inheritance. The waves of our unquiet sea will rise and swell as high as our mountains, and shipwreck the hopes of patriots and the world. For who, then, can rally the nation and roll back the burning tide? Who then can guide the bark of liberty, amid the raging and the roaring of such a sea of fire?

It is idle to say that the enforcement of our wise and equitable *laws* will, without the moral power of the Gospel, ensure our continued prosperity. How can *laws* bind the heart and purify the motives? How can *laws* repress selfishness, or curb ambition, or eradicate voluptuousness and pride? The worst enemies to civil liberty are offenses which human laws can never reach. Human laws are restricted to the government of external actions, and only such actions as are grossly wrong, and which can be proved by competent witnesses; while the great mainsprings of vice and corruption, lying deep within the soul, remain unreached and unchecked. There must then be a profound reverence for Almighty God resting upon the spirit—an inward love of virtue—a solemn regard to the retributions of eternity, or crime and passion will rage in defiance of all law. The streams of corruption, originating in the recesses of the unsanctified heart, will rise and swell until they burst through every barrier, and our glory and our country will sink down amid the vortex of revolutions. Nations are like volcanoes; they contain within their own bowels the seeds of ruin; and if God takes off his hand they will explode, scattering far and wide the fragments of their greatness. "Manners," says Chatham, "have more influence than laws." Public sentiment, especially in a country like ours, is superior to all legislation. For it matters not how good and wholesome may be our written code, it will remain forever a *dead letter* if there be not public virtue in the mass of the people, sufficient to sustain the officers in its execution.

Now, can the diffusion of *knowledge*, the spread of education, of itself, perpetuate our free institutions? There are no moral qualities in intellect. A man may be glittering in all the attractions of wit, and rich in all the gifts of fancy, and still have within him the heart of a demon. Science is a mere instrument which may be turned either to good or bad account. So that, while knowledge does not of itself corrupt, it does not of itself purify. History lifts her venerable voice and declares that those countries and ages that have been most distinguished for the arts and sciences, have also been most conspicuous for voluptuousness and crime, thus showing that the era of moral dissolution may follow close upon that of the highest intellectual culture. At no period were scientific pursuits more popular in France than during her terrible revolution, when blood flowed in streams down the streets of her capital, and crimes, enough to make devils blush, were daily perpetrated under the sacred name of Liberty.

Nor can *national wealth*, of itself, preserve the liberties of our country. From the manner in which our politicians and public men talk, it is evident that they look upon riches as the chief element of national greatness. Hence their frequent and noisy harangues upon the currency, the taxes, the revenues, and trade. But history declares that national opulence has always been deleterious to national virtue—cooling the patriot's ardor, impairing moral principle, weakening both mind and body, and disqualifying men to defend their country.

The history of our present war shows that the poor have been more prompt to rush to the conflict than the rich. All, therefore, that is done to accumulate wealth and stimulate the nation's thirst for gain, is only providing fuel to the flames which will consume us. The greater our wealth, the more speedy our downfall, unless the power of the Gospel come to the rescue, and teach the people self-denial, curb their avarice, inculcate principles of honesty, and hold up the claims of God and of the soul. Where is Babylon, and Athens, and Rome, those ancient depositories of wealth? Their pomp has gone down to the grave, and the noise of their viols has ceased; and from their gray ruins comes up a voice which seems to say: "Let not the wise man glory in his wisdom; let not the mighty man glory in his might; let not the rich man glory in his riches, but let him that glorieth, glory in the Lord." "For the nation and kingdom that will not serve God shall perish; yea, those nations shall be utterly wasted."

Let it then be proclaimed aloud this day, throughout the whole length aud breadth of the land, that nothing but an enlightened public sentiment, under the control of religious principle, can maintain the ascendency over corruption, and preserve our country. Tell us not of our wise legislation, of our patriotism, and of our armies. Tell us not that in a nation like ours, wealth is power, or that talent is power, or that knowledge is power, or that law is power, or that bayonets are power. There is a declaration that must be placed above them all, viz.: *Truth is power*. Wealth cannot purchase it, talent cannot refute it, knowledge cannot overreach it, laws cannot silence it, bayonets cannot crush it. Fling it into the most tremendous billows of popular commotion, cast it into the seven-fold heated furnace of the tyrant's wrath, it will mount aloft like the ark on the waves of the deluge; it will walk like the Son of God, untouched amid the burning fiery furnace. *Truth*—evangelic truth; a profound reverence for Almighty God; a deep sense of personal responsibility, pervading all classes from the lowest to the most exalted, it is this (in conjunction with education and the love of liberty) which will preserve our country, and make it a blessing to our descendants and the world.

And now, in view of all that has been said, let us here pause, and ask ourselves this solemn question: What are we, as a nation, doing to uphold and spread these great principles, which are essential to the perpetuity of our free institutions? How are we acting in view of the fact that "righteousness exalteth a nation," and that the nation and kingdom that will not serve God, shall perish? Have we no national sins to mourn over? Are there no indications among us of an alarming degeneracy? Is there nothing in the signs of the times forcing the conviction upon the Christian patriot's heart, that we, as a people, are forsaking the God of our fathers, and are cherishing in our bosom the seeds of national ruin? Bear in mind that the connection between national sins and national ruin is not arbitrary—it is natural. God does not usually destroy guilty nations by a miracle. The people that will not serve God shall perish, as the legitimate result of their own conduct. They destroy themselves.

And what are some of our national sins? Must we not place prominently in the list the wide-spread desecration of the Sabbath; thousands making the day a season for secular business, or of festivity and gossip; the transaction of official duties under the plea of military necessity; the example of our governors, our judges, our congressmen, and our military officers, who are notorious for their neglect of public worship. Look at intemperance, with its kindred vices of profanity, lewdness, and gambling; the awful increase of conjugal infidelity; military libertines and gaily attired wantons, unblushingly parading all our towns, and jostling honest men's wives and daughters; the growing laxity of family discipline; the withdrawal of the requisite means to support the Gospel, and the conseqent necessity of ministers engaging in secular pursuits to sustain their families; the wide-spread speculations and exorbitant prices in reference to the necessaries of life; the frauds and peculations in our various army bureaux; the corruption of the press; the neglect of the duties of masters to their slaves; the neglect of the families of our brave soldiers who have gone far from home to fight the battles of our country.

Are these some of our national sins? What then must be our doom, unless speedy repentance and reformation interpose? "Shall not the Lord visit for these things, and shall not he be avenged on such a nation as this?" And may he not give us over to our own lusts, a prey? A lingering decay is worse than a sudden overthrow.

A nation dies when everything great and good dies in it. The name may live after the glory has departed. Talk not of our written Constitution, glorious as it is—immortal as we hope it may be. Political security dwells not in the *letter*, but in the *spirit* of our free institutions. Yet many deem all safe, so long as the letter is safe. Death does not take away the soul and body both. Life may have departed, and yet not an artery, or bone, or fiber be removed. And so the *spirit* of a government may perish, and not a line or letter of its written constitution be effaced. When usurpation comes in, masked and hypocritical, its abiding place is usually the dead letter of a once free Constitution.

Behold Augustus Cæsar wielding imperial power amid the forms of a dead republic. The safest place of despotism is the vacant temple of freedom—a woeful desecration, like the temple of God turned into the mart of the money changers.

Finally, I call upon all, in view of our alarming condition, to prostrate themselves before the mighty Ruler of the Universe. Humble yourselves under the mighty hand of God. Be afflicted and mourn and weep. Let your laughter be turned into mourning, and your joy to heaviness. Let your prayer be, "Spare, oh Lord, spare thy people, and give not thy heritage to reproach." Forget not that the sins of the nation are the sins of the individuals who compose it. Let each one, then repent of his personal sins. Let each one enquire how far he has, by his example, contributed to swell the guilt of the land, and excite the wrath of the Almighty.

We read that when Nineveh was threatened by the prophet Jonah, the king proclaimed a fast. "'And he arose from his throne, and he laid his robe from him, and covered himself with sackcloth, and sat in ashes.' And the whole city was clad in the habiliments of sorrow. Yea, the very cattle were deprived of their usual sustenance, that by their mournful lowing, they might increase the solemnity of the occasion. And, in consequence of this public and universal humiliation, the Lord spared the city. If, on this day, set apart as a season of national fasting and prayer, our honored Chief Magistrate, with his distinguished associates in the government, has cast aside the pomp and ceremonials of office, and has prostrated himself in humility before his God, and if a loud and fervent cry for mercy has ascended from a million of penitent hearts in all parts of this bleeding country, may we not humbly trust that our prayers will be heard; that our sins as a nation shall be blotted out, that the judgments of heaven will be arrested, and that rich and abundant blessings such as God alone can bestow, will visit all our borders? 'Then shall the earth yield her increase; and God, even our own God, shall bless us.' "

THE GLORY OF THE CHURCH.

Preached at Bethel Church (near Oakland College), on taking the pastoral charge of said church, April 23, 1843.

"*The King's daughter is all glorious within.*"—Psalm 45:13. This language is figurative. By "the King's daughter" is meant the Church. And by the Church is meant—the body of all true believers of every name and country, however separated by national or ecclesiastical barriers. What, are we informed, constitutes the glory of the Church? Something which is internal. "The King's daughter is all glorious within." Now, if the glory of the universal Church be internal, the glory of every particular branch of the Church must be internal likewise. Because, whatever is true of the whole, must be true of all the several parts. Consequently the glory of every individual Christian, as well as of every particular denomination, is internal glory—the glory of the inner man—a glory arising not from external splendor, but from internal tempers and graces. "The King's daughter is all glorious within." "The kingdom of heaven is not meat and drink, but righteousness, and peace, and joy in the Holy Ghost."

Taking the text as our infallible guide, let us proceed to enquire in what consists the true glory of a particular local church or denomination of Christians.

In what does it *not* consist?

1. It does not necessarily consist in wealth. The possession of ample pecuniary means is not essential to the health or vigor of a particular denomination. The

moral power of a Church is often impaired instead of being increased by the influence of great temporal resources. There are two forms in which a Church may possess wealth. It may consist either in the wealth of its individual members, or in the possession of vested funds. If in the former, these results will most generally follow—a sufficiency of pecuniary means to sustain the Church is obtained without a struggle; consequently there exists no powerful cause to beget a deep sense of dependence on God. The pecuniary burdens of the Church, are, in that case, usually borne by a few. These few, because of their wealth or importance, are strongly tempted to arrogate to themselves dangerous prerogatives, to frown upon their poor brethren, and even to interfere with the pastor in the faithful discharge of his duties. Or, does the wealth of a Church consist in vested funds? Consequences still more injurious are liable to ensue. These funds give rise to a spirit of contention. Various and contradictory are the plans proposed for their disbursement; and hypocritical and designing men often insinuate themselves into the pale of the Church, and pervert these funds from their original purposes. Facts to substantiate these remarks might be easily adduced.

But let a denomination be comparatively poor; let it experience difficulty as it respects its pecuniary concerns, and this very difficulty will prove a benefit. It will beget a sense of dependence of God. It will tend to awake up the energies of the whole Church; to bring into requisition the services of every member, and cause every individual to feel that he is called upon to bear his part of the common burden. And just in proportion to the difficulties to be encountered, and in proportion to the degree in which these difficulties are met and borne by the entire mass of the Church, will the interest which will be awakened, and the energy and vigor which will pervade the entire denomination. For nothing tends more powerfully to cement societies or empires together, than a sense of common weakness, or an apprehension of common danger. And nothing is more calculated to beget a deep interest in any object or possession, than the labor and care which have been bestowed upon it. Comparative poverty, pecuniary difficulties, personal self-denial, often aid materially in building up a Church.

2. The glory of a Church does not consist in members. How often has a feeling of despondency insensibly pervaded a denomination and paralyzed its energies, merely from the fewness of its adherents; from a small membership—a thin audience. And, on the other hand, how frequently have very unholy feelings and sentiments been begotten, from the fact that the Church is large, its members numerous, and its stated services attract crowds of hearers. There is something exceedingly flattering to human pride, in the face of numbers. The consciousness that our cause is popular—that we are enrolled with the majority—that there is a large multitude who are acting in concert with us—is calculated to beget a train of feelings by no means in accordance with the humility of the Gospel. Under such circumstances, the Church is in danger of being caressed merely because it is fashionable. There is great danger, also, that excitement will be mistaken for religion, that persons may be admitted upon very slight inquiry into their qualifications, and that hypocrites and designing persons may enroll themselves among the dominant party, solely from selfish and sinister purposes; until, ere long, the Church, trusting wholly to her own strength, loses sight of her great heavenly reliance. But, on the contrary, what more clearly indicates the sincerity and ster-

ling integrity of a Church? When her friends adhere to her through evil as well as through good report; even when her members are few, when her cause is unpopular, and the world treat her with contempt. Then her friends, few and solitary, cling more closely around her. Then their hearts become knit together as the heart of one man; and trusting not to an arm of flesh, rely more implicitly on the arm of the Lord. Then it is they can plead the promise of Scripture—"Fear not, little flock," "Where two or three are met together in my name, there am I in the midst of them." Oh, it is easy and pleasant to go with the multitude. But to stem the current; to breast the storm; to maintain an attachment to a cause which has but few adherents; it is this which tests the character; it is this which lightens all the Christian graces, and evinces a lofty and magnanimous soul.

3. The glory of a Church does not consist in imposing and attractive forms of worship; in the eloquence of her ministry; in the splendor of her architecture; in the visible impressiveness of her stated ceremonies. History declares that the Church has often flourished most and been most glorious within, when persecuted without; when her members have had to take refuge in caves and mountain-tops from the storms of persecutions. True, there is no essential inconsistency between true piety and impressive external ceremonies. But when does there exist the greatest danger of mistaking mere forms for true religion? of substituting the excitement of the imagination for the devotion of the heart? It is when wealth, and taste, and fashion combine their influence to array Christianity in borrowed plumes beneath the splendid domes of some time-hallowed pile; where the dim religious light streams through carved openings, and architecture and dazzling priestly vestments com-

bine with the solemn music of the full-toned organ, to impart an unearthly grandeur to the scene. There the senses may be feasted while the heart remains untouched. There tears may flow, but not the tears of penitence. There the whole soul may be elevated by a species of ecstasy; and after gazing for an hour upon the gaudy pantomime, return with greater zest to the lusts of pleasure of an irreligious life. Oh, be not deceived; "God is a spirit, and they that worship him must worship him in spirit and in truth."

Having thus briefly dwelt upon the negative part of our subject, we come now to dwell upon its positive import. Having shown in what the glory of the Church does not consist, let us now show in what it does consist. The text declares that it consists in something which is internal. "The king's daughter is all glorious within." 1. The glory of the Church consists in her doctrinal purity: in her being the depository of the truth—the advocate and the guardian of the great leading doctrines of the Gospel. A sound and scriptural creed lies at the foundation of all holy obedience. Where there exists in a Church no doctrinal purity, it is impossible long to maintain holiness of heart and life among her members. There can be no elevated morality where there are no sound religious principles. If we think wrong we will act wrong. The creed and the conduct will always go together. Hence, where a Church is unsound in her doctrines, she will be unsound and unholy in her practice. Hence, God has committed to his Church the sacred principles and ordinances of the Gospel, and the Church is commanded to maintain them at all hazards, and transmit them pure and unadulterated from age to age. To this end, we are commanded to "contend earnestly for the faith once delivered to the saints"—"to buy the truth and sell it not"—"to write it upon our hearts"—"to bind it as frontlets upon our foreheads, and to teach it to our children, and to meditate upon it when we lie down, and when we rise up." When, then, is the "King's daughter all glorious within?" When her ministers and her members proclaim to the world that there is but one living and true God—existing in three persons, the Father, the Son, and the Holy Ghost—that the Scriptures are the only infallible guide of faith and practice—that man is a sinner, lost and ruined by the fall—his whole soul utterly depraved and exposed to the wrath and curse of God—that salvation can be obtained only through the blood of Jesus Christ—that the heart must be regenerated by the power of the Holy Ghost—that man must lead a holy life, or else his profession of religion is vain—"that God has appointed a day in which he will judge the world," "when the Lord Jesus will descend from heaven with a shout," "when the heavens shall pass away, and the elements shall melt with fervent heat." When these great truths are believed in all sincerity—proclaimed from the pulpit with all fidelity, and when they produce a holy influence upon the external conduct of those who believe them, then the glory of the Church will shine forth, and "Zion will arise from the dust, put on her beautiful garments, and appear, fair as the moon, clear as the sun, and terrible as an army with banners."

2. The glory of a church consists in her spirituality—in her cultivation of heart-religion—in her tenderness of feeling, ardor of love, and fervency of devotion. Let none suppose we would exalt mere orthodoxy of creed above the more important possession of experimental godliness. No: faith without works is dead. Such a faith will save no man. It will only deepen his future damnation. "For he that knoweth his Master's will and doeth it not, the same shall be beaten with many

stripes." An orthodox creed without a holy heart, is a mere shadow without substance—a house without a foundation—a dead carcass without an animating principle of life—a palace of ice, beautiful externally, but within it is chilliness and death. "Though I speak with the tongues of men and of angels, and have not charity, I am become as sounding brass, or a tinkling cymbal. And though I have the gift of prophecy, and understand all mysteries, and all knowledge; and though I have all faith, so that I could remove mountains, and have not charity, or love, it profiteth me nothing." And what is this love, to which the apostle attaches such infinite value? Love for communion with God—love for secret prayer—love for the Holy Scriptures—love for the Lord Jesus Christ—love for the ordinances of the Church—love for all true Christians—love for our bitterest enemies. Oh, it is when Christians entertain these feelings, that the Church becomes "all glorious within."

3. The glory of a Church consists in the harmony of its members. "Behold, how good and how pleasant it is for brethren to dwell together in unity! It is like precious ointment upon the head, that ran down upon the beard, even Aaron's beard; that went down to the skirts of his garments; as the dew of Hermon, and as the dew that descended upon the mountains of Zion: for there the Lord commanded the blessing, even life for evermore." Nothing more powerfully illustrates the divinity of our holy religion, than a oneness of feeling, of sentiment, and of action, among its professors. And why should it not be so? How gloriously was this exhibited on the day of Pentecost: "And when the day of Pentecost was fully come, they were all with one accord in one place. And suddenly there came a sound from heaven, as of a rushing mighty wind, and it filled

all the house where they were sitting. And there appeared unto them cloven tongues like as of fire, and it sat upon each of them. And they were all filled with the Holy Ghost, and began to speak with other tongues, as the Spirit gave them utterance." Then was the Church "all glorious within." Christians bore the impress of the divine image in their hearts, and brought forth the fruits of holiness in their lives. Ministers and people felt a common impulse. They had one heart, one hope, and one interest. "The love of Christ constrained them," and losing sight of all party feuds and personal animosities, they were wholly absorbed in one sublime object, the glory of God, and the salvation of the souls of men. And that object was attained. The Holy Ghost came down, and three thousand were added in one day. Now let Christians in our day, unite together in the same harmonious union—let them all come together with one accord, in one place—full of faith, full of zeal, full of brotherly love, and effects as glorious would be sure to follow. The whole united energy of the Church, concentrated in this one grand object, would call down the influences of the spirit of God. A deep solemnity would pervade all classes. But why the low state of piety in the Church? The alienations, the strifes, and the unhallowed divisions of Christians. "One is for Paul, another for Apollos, and few for Christ." One finds fault with the preacher; another complains of being slighted by his brethren; a third is given to a continued spirit of fault-finding; and murmuring, and envyings, and heart-burnings mar the beauty of Zion. "And the Spirit, like a peaceful dove, flees from the scenes of noise and strife."

UNIVERSAL BENEVOLENCE.

An address preached before the Young Men's Christian Association of Houston, August, 1873.

"*As we have, therefore, opportunity, let us do good unto all men; especially to them who are of the household of faith.*"—Galatians, 6 : 10. Those who "are of the household of faith," have special claims upon the benevolence of their brethren; for they have commenced a life of peculiar trials, have espoused a cause to which is often attached peculiar odium, and against which are often arrayed enemies of no common virulence. Hence they need a peculiar and unusual share of fraternal sympathy and aid. From these considerations, however, we are by no means to infer that this class of our fellow-men are to be exclusive objects of our love. We must "do good unto all men." Where'er there is a sufferer throughout the immense brotherhood of man, there must love hover on her downy pinion. Like the knight-errant in the days of chivalry, who roamed the earth to punish proud oppressors, and vindicate the trodden-down rights of the friendless, so must man sally forth with a hand to succor and a heart to feel; prompt to every call of mercy; equipped, as opportunity may present, to dispel ignorance, to soothe sorrow, to reclaim the wanderer from the path of virtue, and wipe the cold sweat from the brow of the dying.

I shall attempt to advocate the claims of universal benevolence. Why must we do good unto all men?

1. Universal benevolence constitutes the true dignity of man.

Under no other garb does human nature present a more sublime aspect. He who is actuated by the expansive spirit of doing good; he who aspires to be not a mere passive recipient, but an active, a munificent distributer of blessings, feels that he is born for a high and noble destiny. Hence he learns to look down with abhorrence upon all that is base, tyrannical, and bigoted. He gradually gains the mastery over his evil passions; bursts the chains of selfishness and pride; overleaps the narrow bounds of sectarian exclusiveness; obtains an effectual antidote against the undue love of money, and throws wide the doors of his heart to the entrance of every generous and philanthropic impulse. Must not that be the most exalted species of human nobleness, which gives birth to feelings and results like these? The possession of this virtue constitutes the true dignity of man, for it leads directly and necessarily to an observance of the holy Decalogue. "Love is the fulfilling of the law." Let universal benevolence become the prevailing temper of the heart. And how can its possessor, for one moment, endure the thought of assailing a fellow-mortal's person, or breathing a whisper of calumny against his reputation, or violating his rights of property, or coveting his dear and most cherished possessions? Benevolence is man's true dignity, for it assimilates him to all the great and noble beings in the universe. It causes him to bear some resemblance to Almighty God. "God is love." His very existence constitutes a boundless ocean of benevolence. It causes him to resemble the Lord Jesus Christ, that glorious Prince of benefactors. It elevates him to a place among the most exalted and renowned spirits that have ever trod the earth—the Washingtons, the La Fayettes, and the Howards; men who lived, and toiled, and wept for the good of their fellow-men; the effects of whose benefactions will be coeval with Time; the measure of whose fame will be boundless as Eternity. It is the spirit of expanded benevolence which lives and breathes through all the works of nature. Every object throughout the vast material universe, seems to exist on purpose to do good, to communicate blessings to other beings, while it apparently makes no provision for itself. The glorious sun, the rolling ocean, the rivers, the silvery mountain streamlet, the many-colored rainbow, the enameled flowers, the dappled morn, the bending fruits of autumn—all, all are continually pouring forth streams of pure beneficence into the lap of man, whilst they take back no blessing in return. All nature is "beauty to the eye, or music to the ear." And will that which gives so much loveliness and grandeur to nature, impart no moral sublimity and dignity to man?

2. Universal benevolence constitutes the true happiness of man.

All those other sources to which mankind usually resort for pleasure—such as fame, wealth, exemption from pain and care—are often very difficult to be found; or if found, are most difficult to be retained; or if retained, and indulged in beyond a certain limit, recoil upon the heart surcharged with a load of remorse, satiety, and disgust. But here is one pure fountain, to which every thirsty soul may have free and unobstructed access. The crystal streams flow perennially. The channel never dries. Of its healthful waters full and frequent draughts may be imbibed, and no loathing disrelish will e'er ensue.

The pleasures of benevolence are of two kinds: *positive* and *negative.* It *creates happiness;* it *prevents misery.* And if the blessing of benevolence was merely of the latter kind, it would constitute the most desirable of all possessions. For, let it once gain entrance into the heart, and how instantaneously will it drive out a legion of diabolical passions—envy, anger, covetousness, revenge—passions that rankle in the heart like barbed arrows, sting like scorpions, gnaw like vultures; and ever and anon bursting forth like the smoldering fires of a hidden volcano, roll their scalding lava over society. But pour the oil of pure philanthropy into the soul, and the billows cease to roll; the storm subsides into a placid calm.

Is this the only species of negative happiness which benevolence occasions? It is not. The God of heaven has so constituted man, that not more than one-half of his existence is absolutely requisite for needful toil, sleep, and animal indulgence. Consequently, as a general rule, every human being has a large surplus of time, talent, and energy, over and above what is necessary for his own use. A very important question then here arises: *How shall this surplusage be employed?* In what way shall it be expended? To what cause shall it be sacredly devoted? Benevolence would gladly step in and borrow it of man; and after having employed it in her sacred service, pour a glorious compensation into the owner's bosom. But man will not accept of the overture. This precious capital, instead of being made to yield a daily revenue of unalloyed pleasure, is most wickedly perverted; and by being so, generates a countless train of woes. "What shall we do to get rid of this useless portion of our existence? how shall we kill time?" is the constant aim of multitudes.

One seems to aspire to no higher honor than the life of a mere animal. He has eat and drank and slept like a stall-fed ox, until at last he can endure it no longer. And linked to his species by no strong ties of sympathetic feeling, absorbed and elevated by no grand object of pursuit, life becomes an intolerable burden; the world, a gloomy prison-house; and raising his suicidal hand, he plunges the dagger to his own heart, and rushes unbidden into eternity. Another has too great dread of death, thus suddenly to let go his hold on life. But still, he has unoccupied time and unemployed energies, which hang heavy on his hands; and what shall he do with them? He turns lazy monk, or musing anchorite. Behold a third. He has spent many a year of toil and care, to accumulate wealth. At last he has attained his object. And now what shall he do with the remainder of his days? How shall he enjoy his dear-bought possessions? Oh, this he will do: he will retire from business, and having bought him a beautiful villa far from the bustling throng, he will there doze out the remainder of his days in calm retirement—a second Cincinnatus or Sage of Monticello; forgetting, however, that he has no fountains of enjoyment, as they had, in his own breast. And no sooner, then, is he fairly housed in his new retreat, than he falls a prey to the most morbid melancholy; and unless he speedily retake himself to his former bustling occupation, he will die of premature old age, or sink into all the whims and frailties of a second childhood. Behold a fourth. He is determined that *he* will not die, like his purse-proud neighbor, of gout or ennui; but will keep on at the goodly and respectable occupation of making money. Wan and care-worn, he pursues his ceaseless round—counts his bags and cons his ledger; until at last he falls a victim to a most wretched monomania; avarice lays her cold clutches upon his stinted soul; *money, money*, is his god—"give, give," like the horse-leech's daughter. And finally, death tears him from his idol, and throws his worthless body to the worms. There is still another, perhaps somewhat singular in the plan *he* adopts, to squander the precious surplus capital with which nature hath endowed him:

"This is your modern man of fashion—
A man of taste and dissipation:
A busy man without employment,
A happy man without enjoyment.
In sleep, and dress, and sport, and play,
He throws his worthless life away.
Has no opinion of his own,
But takes from leading beaux the ton.
Custom pursues, his only rule,
And lives an ape and dies a fool."

Now what a blessed antidote to all these miserable modes of dragging out life, of murdering existence, does benevolence propose. Take that surplus of time, talent, and energy, which you do not need for your own wants, and the squandering of which causes so much sin and folly, and expend it in the cause of others. "Go about doing good." Open thine eyes upon a world of misery. Instruct the ignorant, reclaim the vicious, espouse the cause of the friendless. Seek out retiring merit and unrequited virtue from their secret abodes, and demand for them a public reward. Aid in sending the Gospel to the heathen. Oh, let the wail of the orphan and the tears of the widow—let the piteous tale of the penniless, the groans that issue from dungeons and battle-fields, from families escaping from their blazing habitations, and mariners wrecked upon the ocean, reach thine ears, and pierce thine heart, and nerve thy soul to noble deeds of charity. Then thine energies will never stagnate; then thy sympathies in life will never expire for want of nutriment; then thou wilt never become a prey to melancholy, nor life hang heavy on thy hands, because of no great object of pursuit to give healthful occupation to thy powers.

Such are some of the mere *negative* portions of the pleasures of benevolence. But, in addition to all this, she has happiness of a *positive* kind, joys of her own creation, pure fountains in the heart, of which none can taste but their own possessor. For there is the fervent prayer of the poor; there is the tear of gratitude trickling down the cheek; and the heart-felt invocation of heaven's richest blessing on thy soul, uttered by him thou hast so timely succored. There, too, is the joy of giving, the luxury of doing good, sweeter to the soul than music's richest melody, or the gush of water in the desert to the thirsty pilgrim. Oh, if there be a foretaste of angel's food on earth, it is the consciousness of having done a noble action, of having dried a mourner's tears, or stanched one bleeding wound in sorrow's breast.

> "This world's *not* 'all a fleeting show,
> For man's illusion given;'
> He that hath soothed a widow's woe,
> Or wiped an orphan's tears, doth know
> There is something here of heaven."

"It is more blessed to give than to receive." "The liberal soul shall be made fat; and he that watereth, shall be watered also himself." While he that has no boon to bestow upon his species, is the meanest of all God's creatures. He has no music in his soul. He is

> "Creation's blot, creation's blank;
> Whom none can love, whom none can thank."

Power will cause you to be feared; learning, to be admired; wealth and beauty, to be flattered. But naught but benevolence will cause you to be truly loved. And when thou diest, tears of gratitude will be poured out like sweet incense on thy tomb, and children yet unborn shall lisp with reverence thy name.

3. The virtue which we advocate is the very essence of true piety.

In proof of this position, hear the plain and positive declarations of God's word. 1 John 4 : 20: "If a man say, I love God, and hateth his brother, he is a liar; for he that loveth not his brother whom he hath seen, how can he love God whom he hath not seen?" James 2 : 15, 16: "If a brother or sister be naked, and destitute of daily food; and one of you say unto them, depart in peace, be ye warmed, and filled; notwithstanding ye give them not those things which are needful to the body; what doth it profit?" "Pure religion and undefiled before God and the Father is this, to visit the fatherless and widows in their affliction, and to keep one's self unspotted from the world." And at the awful day of judgment, after the glorious temple of truth and righteousness, which is now erecting on this earth, shall have received its completion, and "Grace, Grace," shall be the shout of heaven's anthem at the laying of the top-stone, and when the mighty Architect shall come down to review the work, and knock away this external scaffolding, and pay off the laborers, "then shall he sit upon the throne of his glory; and before him shall be gathered all nations; and he shall separate them one from another, as a shepherd divideth his sheep from the goats. And he shall set the sheep on the right hand, but the goats on the left. Then shall the King say to them on his right hand, Come ye blessed of my Father, inherit the kingdom prepared for you from the foundation of the world. For I was an hungered, and ye gave me meat; I was thirsty, and ye gave me drink; I was a stranger, and ye took me in; naked, and ye clothed me; I was sick, and ye visited me; I was in prison, and ye came unto me. Then shall the righteous (bowed down with a sense of their great unworthiness and many imperfections) answer him, saying, Lord, when saw we thee an hungered, and fed thee? or thirsty, and gave thee drink? When saw we thee a stranger, and took thee in? or naked, and clothed thee? or when saw we thee sick, or in prison, and came unto thee? And the King shall answer, and say unto them, Verily I say unto you, inasmuch as ye done it unto one of the least of these my brethren, ye have done it unto me." (For the poor are my representatives on earth. I myself was once a homeless wanderer; and while the foxes had holes, and the birds of the air had nests, the son of man had not where to lay his head.)

The awards of the great day, you perceive, will turn upon the discharge or neglect of these six charities. The Judge then will not ask, "Have ye possessed mere cold and heartless orthodoxy, or flaming zeal? Have ye punctiliously adhered to certain rites and ceremonies, or contended with unseemly warmth for ecclesiastical order. But, more than all this, have ye fed the hungry? have ye clothed the naked? have ye given water to the thirsty soul? sheltered the houseless stranger? soothed the moaning anguish of the sick? and visited the prisoner in his dungeon?"

"Abou Ben Adhem (may his tribe increase!)
Awoke one night from a deep dream of peace
And saw, within the moonlight in his room,
Making it rich, and like a lily in bloom,
An angel writing in a book of gold:—
Exceeding peace had made Ben Adhem bold,
And to the angel in the room he said,
'What writest thou?' The vision raised its head,
And with a look made of all sweet accord,
Answer'd, 'The names of those who love the Lord.'
'And is mine one?' asked Abou. 'Nay, not so,'
Replied the angel. Abou spoke more low,
But cheerly still; and said, 'I pray thee, then,
Write me as one that loves his fellow-men.'
The angel wrote, and vanish'd. The next night
It came again, with a great wakening light,

> And show'd the names whom love of God had bless'd,
> And lo! Ben Adhem's name led all the rest."

4. Universal benevolence is strongly inculcated from taking into consideration the identity of the human race.

"And who is my neighbor?" Where are the members of my fraternity? Oh, I see one, shivering amidst the snows of Greenland; another, wrapt in furs amidst the smoke of his Norwegian cottage; a third, wading with the weary caravan over the burning sands of Sahara's desert. I recognize my brother in that sable form, musing in plaintive mood, amidst the gray ruins of Babel or of Tadmor; in that naked savage, chasing the deer up the steeps of the Rocky Mountains, far towards the setting sun.

Therefore we would enforce the exhortation of the text: "Let us do good unto *all men*," from the fact that all men are brethren.

> "Ne'er withdraw thy pity from thy brother:
> ——————Whatsoe'er his garb
> Or lineament may be; howe'er the sun
> Hath burnt dark tints upon him, or the yoke
> Of vassalage and scorn hath bowed him low—
> Still must thy spirit at thy brother's pain,
> Vibrate as the swept lyre."

5. Universal benevolence is most solemnly inculcated, by considering the great benefits and blessings which would flow from its universal prevalence.

Is it not enough to make one "blush and hang his head to think himself a man," when he reflects upon the mighty talents, the transcendent capabilities with which God hath endowed the race, and which, instead of being made to subserve the cause of virtue, have been used to scathe and desolate the earth? Oh, to what a peerless height of bliss and beauty would this world have long ago aspired, had all our great men been good men; had men of might been men of God; had Alexander the Great been a missionary of mercy; had Julius Cæsar crossed the Rubicon as a herald of salvation; had Napoleon Bonaparte vowed upon his bended knees before high heaven, that he would rush to the rescue of his suffering fellow-men, and no more revisit the blushing vinehills of his lovely France until he had penetrated the icy regions of the North, crossed the frozen Alps, doubled the stormy Cape, and planted the standard of light and love amid the teeming millions of the East.

But what would be the inevitable results flowing from the prevalence of universal love? Wars would cease. National jealousies would expire. Dueling would be known merely as the relic of a dark and murderous age. The dishonorable and cowardly practice of carrying concealed weapons would meet with one loud, long hiss of scorn. Lawless ambition, political oppression, slander, disobedience to parents, falsehood, theft, conjugal infidelity, sectarian exclusiveness, all would expire. And from earth's regenerated energies would spring forth a glorious harvest of every generous and noble virtue. Then every hovel of distress would be visited, every afflicted and persecuted soul would find a friend, every debt would be punctually paid, every commodity sold at its real value, every article of merchandise exhibited in its true light, every promise faithfully kept, every dispute amicably adjusted, every man's character held in sacred estimation. Oh, glorious era!

"Lord, for those days we wait—those days
Are in thy word foretold:—
Fly swifter, sun and stars, and bring
That promised age of gold."

MORAL INSANITY.

Preached at Vicksburg, 1841.

"*I am not mad, most Noble Festus.*"—Acts 26 : 25. The learned Paul was esteemed a maniac. And in reference to one greater than Paul, it was said, "he is beside himself." And how often has the same charge been brought against ardent Christians in our own day. —Glowing zeal for the truth, devout reverence for God, pungent sorrow for sin, occasional rapture of devotion, or uncommon fervor in prosecuting some great scheme of benevolence, have often been viewed as evidences of mental derangement. But is the charge just? Let us examine and see. Mental derangement usually exhibits itself in the form of *monomania*—*i. e.*, derangement upon some particular topic, while on all other themes the mind retains its equilibrium. None but *idiots* manifest entire mental fatuity. It is only when unduly occupied by some one train of thought, or when indulging in some darling passion, or when prosecuting with intemperate ardor some favorite object of pursuit, that the intellect becomes unsettled. Hence, it is a most rare phenomenon, to meet with an individual frenzied or insane, whose business or situation in life requires him frequently to change his trains of thought, or to pass, in pleasant transition, from one occupation to another. And it is a fact of frequent occurrence, that those who have lost their intellectual balance, have found immediate relief from a change of scenery or occupation—from traveling, music, literary pursuits, or the conversation of persons of sprightly conversational powers.

Now, if such be the cause, and such the cure of mental alienation, how can experimental religion ever make a man a maniac? Experimental piety, wherever healthful and scriptural, precludes entire and undivided absorption in one train of thought or one species of emotions, to the exclusion of all others. It calls into exercise a great variety of mental powers, and gives indulgence to every species of emotions and pursuits. Does it create fears, it also creates hopes. Hath it sorrows, it hath also joys. Does it inculcate gravity, it likewise enjoins cheerfulness. Does it demand attention to the concerns of the soul, it is equally explicit in enforcing attention to the claims of the body. Does it call for the exercise of love to God, it is equally pointed in commanding love to man. Let then the religion of the Gospel exert its legitimate power upon the mind and heart, and it will serve as a complete system of *checks and balances*, precluding, in its very nature, everything like mental insanity. The thoughts it begets, the feelings it enkindles, the duties and pursuits it inculcates, are too *diversified* to lead to such a result.

But experimental religion is not only not the *cause* of insanity, it is often its *cure*, or its *preventive*—"ministering to a mind diseased, and plucking from the heart a rooted sorrow." Religion forbids violent grief, and violent anger—excessive mirth or excessive melancholy—frantic wailings for the dead, or wild bursts of joy at the sudden attainment of wealth or honor. It pacifies a guilty conscience, removes the pangs of remorse, curbs the fiend-like passion of revenge, imparts contentment to the lot assigned by Providence, and removes the terrors of death. Oh, how often have we known it to come suddenly to the rescue, like an angel of mercy, seizing the stricken spirit from the grasp of some foul fiend, and preventing the lunatic's vacant stare, the maniac's gloom, or the madman's frenzy. Therefore, can that which prevents insanity, ever cause it? Can the antidote become the bane? "Can the same fountain send forth salt water and fresh."

A celebrated medical gentleman, at the head of an English lunatic asylum, has informed the world, that "moral impulses very rarely produce insanity." And he states that he came to this conclusion from the sedulous treatment of nearly 700 cases of the disease, only one individual of which number had become insane from a religious cause. He had frequently been informed that some particular patient had become religiously insane. But whenever he had obtained an intelligent history of the case, he uniformly found that the individual had exhibited symptoms of insanity, before he became a religious devotee.

LOVE OF MONEY.

Missionary Address in New Orleans, 1860.

How universal and idolatrous is the estimate which mankind attach to money! Although there is no possession more uncertain, none more destructive of peace of mind, none more productive of crime and prodigality among children, yet there is nothing after which the majority of men grasp more eagerly, and for which they are willing to make greater sacrifices, than for this. The Scriptures declare that "the love of money is the root of all evil," *i. e.*, all kinds of evil have had their origin in the love of money. There is no species of evil, whether physical or mental, which has not, at some time or other, originated here. The sin of covetousness is, in some respects, the most heinous and dangerous sin of which man is liable.—It is so, not merely on account of its direct and positive effects, but also because of the many plausible and winning aspects which it is capable of assuming. It can transform itself into an angel of light. Under the commendable plea of taking care of the family, or laying up in store for old age, or providing something for the cause of charity, it can impose upon the most cautious, until it finally takes entire possession of the soul. Covetousness is almost the only sin which is tolerated in decent society. Profaneness, drunkenness, and sensuality must often hide their heads; while covetousness, because of its genteel and frugal aspects, rears its head unrebuked and unabashed. Covetousness is the only sin which is tolerated in the Church. A professing Christian dare not be grossly immoral, but he dare be covetous. As the loss of one of the five senses renders the others more acute, so, the giving up of the common and grosser forms of vice, by some persons, when they become members of the Church, imparts to this darling sin a tenfold power. And while men of the world commit all sins without restraint, covetous members of the Church concentrate their corrupt nature upon this one. Hence it becomes intense, absorbing. The moral power of the Church is lowered, her energies are crippled, and multitudes bow down before the shrine of Mammon. Bunyan tells of some pilgrims, who, on their journeying to the Heavenly City, were induced to turn aside from their road, to look at a silver mine, recently discovered in a little hill called "Lucre." "Now," says the great dreamer, "whether they went down therein to dig or were choked by the fumes that arose from the bottom, I know not. But they were never heard of afterwards." O Christian, beware of "covetousness, which is idolatry." Let the case of the rich young man, "who went away sorrowful, because he had great possession"—let the fate of Achan, who "perished not alone in his iniquity"—of Judas, who sold his Master "for thirty pieces of silver"—of Ananias and Sapphira, who "kept back part of the possession" and "lied unto the Holy Ghost," serve as solemn warnings of danger.

INFLUENCE.

"*For none of us liveth to himself.*—Romans 14 : 7. Human beings are linked together by indissoluble ties. They are virtuous or vicious in groups. They rise and fall in masses. Every one is surrounded by a species of atmosphere. This atmosphere others breathe, and by it others are affected. Hence, the impulse given either to truth or error, by a single individual, may be felt throughout a whole nation, and affect unborn generations: "For none of us liveth to himself, and no man dieth to himself." None can isolate himself from his race and move on in an independent sphere. On the contrary, we are continually *radiating* images of ourselves, which others see and others feel. All men have an influence. The good and the bad have each an influence. How do bad men acquire their influence?

1. Precept gives them influence. They lead others to do wrong, by *teaching* to do wrong. This is done much more extensively than many suppose. Without boldly advocating palpable errors or admitted crimes, at which the moral sense of the community would be shocked, bad men often gain their object by a method less obvious but not less effectual. They inculcate a lax but plausible system of morality. They talk lightly of the sanctions of the Divine law, and thus weaken its hold on the hearts of the young. They talk disparagingly of conscience, and represent its secret admonitions as

the effects of an early education or the offspring of a morbid sensibility. And thus their associates, ere they are aware of it, have imbibed a poison more deadly than the viper's tooth. The moral sense is blunted. The distinction between right and wrong is obliterated. Corrupt principles of action are instilled, and vice is soon practiced instead of virtue. How plausible and how smooth-tongued is often the teacher of error! He professes a profound reverence for truth. None more rigid in contending for principles than he. He would sooner cut off his right arm than teach a falsehood or advocate a crime. And while he dare not openly attack the gates of the citadel, he, in his way, slyly undermines the foundations. He secures the outposts, bribes the sentinels, and, by allaying all suspicion, more effectually gains an entrance. Vice is always more dangerous when clothed in the garb of virtue, and the errorist when arrayed in the panoply of truth. The most successful knaves come thus disguised, as smooth as razors dipped in oil, but as sharp.

2. Example gives influence. Wicked men usually accompany their sophistical reasonings by a corrupt practice. This gives authority to their precepts, and renders them tenfold more dangerous. They who are at first shocked at a bad man's principles may insensibly fall in love with his example; and, following at first at a respectful distance, may gradually approach nearer, until at length they become his bosom companions, his obsequious imitators. For it is not the example of the most vicious and abandoned which is the most corrupting. The drunkard who wallows in the mire may be abhorred, while the more temperate drinker may have a host of imitators. The bold blasphemer may be viewed as a public nuisance, while the polite skeptic, the gay sportsman, the accomplished man of pleasure, may have

troops of friends and give tone to the whole community. Some serpents are gifted with the power of fascination. They first charm their victim ere they strike their fang. And so it is with some men. Their example is a gilded one. They attract by their manners, they win by their eloquence, they overawe the censures of the good by their popularity and wealth. And at last, when they die, a vast multitude of the young, the amiable, and the inexperienced will rise up in the judgment and heap curses on their heads as the authors of their ruin.

3. Age gives influence. The precepts and example of an old man, whether upon the side of vice or virtue, always have more weight than those of a younger one. An old man has lived longer. He has had more experience, and is better acquainted with the world. His gray hairs are reverenced. He has more authority. He has his family circle and connections around him. While, then, it is true that "one sinner destroyeth much good," this is peculiarly true of an old sinner. Here you behold the case of one, the combined influence of whose entire life has been polluting a whole family and a whole neighborhood. The companions of his youth, the children and associates of his riper years, as well as the familiar companions of his declining days—a large multitude, have all been breathing his corrupting atmosphere, have been inhaling the slow poison of his contaminating influence.

4. Exalted station gives influence. When the fountains are corrupt, the streams are always impure. Rulers have an influence which the people have not. Public men frame our laws, and are the models by which multitudes shape their opinions and their conduct. Wide and fearful, then, is the prevalence of vice, when public men are corrupt. They send forth streams of impurity to the extremities of the land, corrupt the fountains of

justice, and bring a whole nation under the curse of Heaven, causing thousands to perish in their sins, like the vessel freighted with a precious cargo of human life, which is dashed against the rocks through the negligence of a drunken pilot, and all go down together.

5. The domestic relations give influence. Yea, this is the chief source of influence. It is here, where almost all that is good or ill in human life has its origin. It is around the domestic hearth that piety and every noble virtue begin to grow. It is by the domestic fireside that youth are trained up to be their country's ornament or their country's scourge. It is from the family that heaven and hell are peopled. If rulers have an influence over the people, parents exert a tenfold greater influence over their children, husbands over wives, and brothers and sisters over each other. As is the parent, so is the child. As are the associations of early life, so are the sentiments of riper years. If parents sow the seeds of piety, inculcate principles of goodly living, "allure to brighter worlds and lead the way," children are almost sure to follow. But if parents inculcate no good sentiments, crush no vicious propensities, set no godly example, use no efforts to ward off those countless unhallowed influences which prowl around the domestic enclosure, how, under such circumstances, can piety obtain a lodgment in the youthful bosom? You might as well expect roses to bloom upon a mountain of snow. Such are some of the causes of that mysterious power which every human being, even the humblest, is continually exerting over the circle in which he moves. Every utterance of the lips, every action of the life, the whole force of example, the station occupied, the relation sustained, whether of ruler, friend, teacher, parent, husband, wife, or child, is casting an image upon some fellow mortal, and is influencing him for good or evil. It

is evident, then, that no one is sufficiently aware of his influence. An indiscreet remark, made in thoughtlessness or excitement, may have formed the germ of vice in some youthful bosom, and may bring forth fruit unto death, long after he who uttered it has passed away from earth. Reader, what is your influence? Is it salutary? Your example, is it safe? Your vowed principles, are they sound? Remember, you are in a certain sense your brother's keeper. You cannot prevent your influence. *It will be felt.*

SEMI-CENTENNIAL

OF

PRESBYTERIANISM IN NEW ORLEANS.

In accordance with previous notice, the Presbyterian congregations assembled in the First Presbyterian Church, on Lafayette square, on last Sabbath evening, to celebrate, with appropriate services, the organization of the first Presbyterian church in this city, on the twenty-third of November, fifty years ago.

The pulpit and its surroundings were tastefully decorated with floral wreaths and emblems, suited to the occasion. To the right of the pulpit was the single name—"Larned"—and to the left—"Palmer"—in evergreen letters; with a wreath (also of evergreen) underneath each. On a line with, and between the two, were the figures 1823 and 1873, with a hyphen between the dates; thus joining together as one, the names and years which this memorial day celebrated. The letters were about twelve inches in length, and the figures eighteen. The latter were made of pure chrysanthemums, and looked charming in their rich whiteness.

Upon the communion table, in front of the pulpit, was a mound of flowers, three feet high by three wide, surrounded by evergreens; typical of the names and dates, the past and the present, the living and the dead—erected out of respect to the memory of the founder of the church, and also in honor of the present, living occupant, erected no less to commemorate the lapse of half a century of time between the two.

The chancel rails, pillars of the candelabras, and front of the pulpit platform were festooned with wreaths of evergreens, intermingled with flowers, while cedars and exotic plants were interspersed within and around the altar—altogether creating a beautiful though chaste and solemn effect.

THE SERVICES.

The services were opened precisely at seven o'clock with a beautiful voluntary from the choir.

Rev. B. Wayne, then read the 48th Psalm.

A fervent and impressive prayer was offered by Rev. James Beattie.

Dr. Palmer then read the following narrative:

AN HISTORICAL PAPER ON THE ORIGIN AND GROWTH OF PRESBYTERIANISM IN THE CITY OF NEW ORLEANS.

It is a little remarkable that the first successful effort to plant Presbyterianism in the city of New Orleans should have originated with the Congregationalists of New England. Near the beginning of the year 1817, the Rev. Elias Cornelius was appointed by the Connecticut Missionary Society, to engage in a missionary tour through the southwestern States, more especially to visit New Orleans, then containing a population of thirty to thirty-four thousand, and with but one Protestant minister, the Rev. Dr. Hull; to examine its moral condition, and, while preaching the Gospel to many who seldom heard it, to invite the friends of the Congregational or Presbyterian Communion to establish a church, and secure an able and faithful pastor. In this tour, Dr. Cornelius acted also as agent for the A. B. C. F. M., to solicit funds for the evangelization of the Indian tribes. In this work he was eminently successful—devoting an entire year to a lengthened tour from Massachusetts to Louisiana—collecting large sums for the American Board, and arrived in New Orleans on December 30, 1817.

The most important service rendered by Dr. Cornelius, however, was that of introducing the Rev. Sylvester Larned to this field of labor. In passing through New Jersey, on his journey southward, Dr. Cornelius formed the acquaintance of Mr. Larned, then finishing his divinity course at Princeton, and giving, in the reputation acquired as a student, brilliant promise of a successful career as a preacher. The arrangement was there formed between the two, that Mr. Larned should follow Dr. Cornelius to New Orleans after he should have passed his trials, and should have been admitted to the ministry.

On July 15, 1817, Mr. Larned was licensed and ordained by the Presbytery of New York. This ordination was clearly to the office of Evangelist, which he was in the fullest sense of the word. It appears, too, that the General Assembly of the Presbyterian Church was brought into co-operation with this scheme; from the fact that Drs. Nott and Romeyn were appointed by that body to accompany Mr. Larned to the southwest. This appointment was not, however, fulfilled, and we find the young evangelist, after a brief visit to his native home, leaving on September 26, and journeying alone to the field where he was to gather the laurels of an unfading reputation, and then to sanctify it by an early death. He reached his destination after innumerable delays, January 22, 1818.

Through the antecedent preparation of his friend, Dr. Cornelius, who had preceded him exactly three weeks—and still more by his own splendid attractions—overtures were soon made to him for a permanent settlement. Subscriptions were circulated for the building of a church edifice, which, by April 5, amounted to $16,000. It was proposed, as soon as the subscriptions were completed, to negotiate a loan of $40,000, the estimated cost of a building sixty feet by ninety, with about two thousand sittings. Considering the infancy of the enterprise, the largeness of these plans betokens great vigor of effort, and the confidence felt of final success in collecting and maintaining a flourishing church. In this costly undertaking, generous assistance was received from the City Council, in the grant of two lots of ground valued at $6,000, and in a subsequent loan of $10,000. In the erection of the building, Mr. Larned's spiritual labors were interrupted during the summer of 1818 by a visit north, for the purpose of soliciting money, and also of purchasing materials for building.

On January 8, 1819, the corner-stone of the new edifice was laid with imposing ceremonies (and in the presence of an immense throng), on the selected site on St. Charles street, between Gravier and Union, and on July 4, following, was solemnly dedicated to the worship of Almighty God—with a discourse from Psalms 48 : 9: "We have thought of thy loving kindness, O God, in the midst of thy temple," which will be found the fourth in the series of sermons published in connection with Mr. Larned's Memoirs.

There are no records from which to learn the spiritual growth of the church during this early period, except that in one of his letters, Mr. Larned speaks of a communion season about the middle of July, 1820, in which there were *forty-two* at the table of the Lord, part of whom were, however, Methodists. Mr. Larned's labors were those exclusively of an evangelist; and his brief life was spent in gathering a congregation and building a house of worship. There is no record of his having organized a church according to our ecclesiastical canons, by the election and ordination of ruling elders; and he himself was never installed into the pastoral relation by ecclesiastical authority. It pleased the Great Head of the Church to arrest his labors before they reached this point of consummation. During the month of August, 1820, the scourge which has so often desolated our city, made its appearance. On Sabbath, August 27, he preached from Phil. 1:21, "For me to live is Christ, and to die is gain;" words alas! prophetic of his speedy call to those mansions where all is "gain" forever to the believer. On the following Thursday, August 21, the very day on which he completed the twenty-fourth year of his age, he fell asleep in Jesus—or rather awoke to the glory and joy of his Lord. His remains were consigned to the tomb in Girod Cemetery, with the Episcopal service for the dead rendered by the Rev. Dr. Hull.

Mr. Larned's successor, after an interval of eighteen months, was the Rev. Theodore Clapp, a native of Massachusetts, and a graduate of Yale College, and of the Theological Seminary at Andover. He was licensed by a Congregational Association, October, 1817; and was led providentially to Kentucky, by an engagement as private tutor in a family residing near Lexington, in that State. During the summer of 1821, he spent a few weeks at a watering place in Kentucky, and on the Sabbath preached in one of the public rooms of the hotel to the assembled guests. This apparently casual circumstance led to his settlement in New Orleans. Amongst his hearers on that occasion, were two gentlemen from our city, trustees of Mr. Larned's church; who, upon their return home, caused a letter to be written, inviting him to New Orleans. This invitation, at first declined, led to a visit to this city near the close of February, 1822.

On the third Sabbath after his arrival, he was unanimously chosen to fill the vacant pulpit. Finding the church embarrassed by a debt of $45,000, he naturally hesitated, and finally made its liquidation the condition of his acceptance of the call. The method adopted for this purpose, though deemed proper at the time, would now be disallowed by the better educated conscience of the Church. The trustees made application to the Legislature of Louisiana, then in session, for a lottery; which being sold to Yates & McIntyre of New York, for $25,000, relieved the pressure of debt to that amount. For the remaining $20,000 the building was sold to Judah Touro, Esq., a merchant of wealth, whose magnificent charities have left his name in grateful remembrance to the people of New Orleans. It may be well to state here, though a little in advance of dates, that Mr. Touro held the building to the time of its destruction by fire; allowing the income from pew-rents to the use of the minister, and incurring the expense of keeping it in repair. He was Mr. Clapp's personal friend and benefactor throughout life; and when the original building was burnt, and long after it had been carried away from Presbyterians by Mr. Clapp's secession, Mr. Touro, we believe, built a small chapel for the Unitarian congregation, until a larger edifice could be erected for their accommodation. Such instances of princely munificence deserve to be engraved upon tablets of marble. But this is to anticipate.

The first notice of the organization of this church, as a spiritual body, is in the record of a meeting held for this purpose on November 23, 1823. Prior to this, the labors of Mr. Larned, extending over a period of two years and seven months, from January 22, 1818, to August 31, 1820; and those of Mr. Clapp over a period of one year and nine months, from March, 1822, to November, 1823, were simply evangelistic. A congregation had been gathered, a house of worship built, the word and sacrament administered, and the materials collected for the spiritual Church in the admission of persons to sealing ordinances; all in the exercise of that power which the Scriptures and our Presbyterian standards assign to the evangelist. The time had now arrived for the gathering up the results of these labors in a permanent and organized form.

On the evening of November 23, 1823, just fifty years ago, at a meeting moderated by Rev. Mr. Clapp, nine males and fifteen females presented credentials of having been admitted to the sacrament of the Lord's supper, by Mr. Larned, as follows:

Males:—Alfred Hennen, James Robinson, William Ross, Robert H. McNair, Moses Cox, Hugh Farrie, Richard Pearse, John Spittal, John Rollins. *Females:* —Phebe Farrie, Catherine Hearsey, Celeste Hearsey, Doza A. Hearsey, Margaret Agur, Ann Ross, Eliza Hill, Margaret McNair, Sarah Ann Harper, Ann Davison, Stella Mercer, Jane Robinson, Eliza Baldwin, Mary Porter, Eliza Davidson.

These persons, twenty-four in all, were formed into a church by the adoption of the Presbyterian standards in doctrine, government, discipline, and worship; and by a petition to the Presbytery of Mississippi to be enrolled among the churches under its care, with the style and title of "The First Presbyterian Church in the city and parish of New Orleans." The organization was completed by the election on the same evening of four persons to be ruling elders, viz.: William Ross, Moses Cox, James Robinson, and Robert H. McNair, who were accordingly ordained and installed on the following Sabbath, November 30, 1823.

Mr. Clapp's ministry was a troubled one, from suspicions entertained of his doctrinal soundness. From his own statements, as early as 1824, his faith was shaken as to the doctrine of the eternity of future punishment. He pushed his investigations, doubts darkening upon him, through years, until at length he was forced to plant himself in open hostility to the whole Calvinistic Theology. It is not strange that inconsistent and wavering statements of truth should find their way into the ministrations of the pulpit, at the very time his faith was shaken in the tenets which he had subscribed, and when his own mind was working to an entire renunciation of them. A single crack in a bell is sufficient to destroy its tone; and it is not surprising that some of his parishioners should miss that clear ring which the pulpit is expected to give forth. Certain it is, that the repose of the church was seriously disturbed for years by two parallel prosecutions before the Session against two prominent members of the church, one of them a ruling elder, grounded upon their undisguised dissatisfaction with the minister. In the course of these complicated proceedings, the Session, by death and deposition from offices, became reduced below a constitutional quorum; which led, in March, 1828, to the election and ordination of five new elders, Alfred Hennen, Joseph A. Maybin, William W. Caldwell, Josiah Crocker, and Fabricius Reynolds.

On March 5, 1830, Mr. Clapp addressed a letter to the Presbytery of Mississippi, in which he says, "I have not found, and I at present despair of finding any text of Holy Writ to prove unanswerably the distinguishing tenets of Calvinism." He, therefore, solicited a dismission from the Presbytery to the Hampshire County Association of Congregational ministers in the State of Massachusetts. This dismission was refused by the Presbytery, on the ground that it was inconsistent to dismiss, in good standing, to another body one whom they could no longer recognize in their own; and they proceeded to declare Mr. Clapp no longer a member of their body, or a minister in the Presbyterian Church. A letter was also addressed to the church advising them of this action, and declaring the pulpit vacant. No definite action was taken upon this communication of the Presbytery until January, 1831, when the Session proposed to take the mind of the church, whether to retain Mr. Clapp as their pastor, or to abide by the decision of the Presbytery and to sever that connection. This sifting process was, however, arrested by an exception taken against this action and against the Presbyterial decree upon which it was based. By common consent, the case was carried over the intermediate court immediately to the General Assembly, which body sustained the exception, declaring "that, as Mr. Clapp had neither been dismissed nor suspended by the Presbytery, he ought to be regarded as a member of that body, and that in the opinion of the Assembly, they have sufficient reasons for proceeding to try him upon the charge of error in doctrine."

The case being thus remanded to the Presbytery, had to be taken up anew. Meanwhile the agitation in the bosom of the church could not be allayed. On January 13, 1832, fifteen members, including elders McNair and Caldwell, were dismissed at their request, for the purpose of forming another church upon the principles of the doctrine and discipline of the Presbyterian Church. This seceding body worshiped in a warehouse of Mr. Cornelius Paulding, opposite Lafayette square, on the site covered by the building in which we are now assembled. It enjoyed the services of the Rev. Mr. Harris; but the references to it are scant, and after a brief and flickering existence, its elements were reabsorbed into the First Church. Meanwhile the Presbytery concluded its proceedings in the trial of Mr. Clapp, on January 10, 1833; when he was deposed from the office of the ministry, and his relations to the church, which had only been those of a stated supply and not of an installed pastor, were finally canceled. The roll of communicants, just before the secession in 1832, numbered *eighty-nine.*

Presbyterianism had now to start anew, from a beginning quite as small as at first. The social and amiable qualities of Mr. Clapp endeared him greatly as a man; the large majority of his hearers could not appreciate this clamor about doctrine; and many of the truly pious were slow to credit the extent of his departure from the faith, and were disposed to sympathize with him as one unkindly persecuted. The few, therefore, who came forth, exactly nine, with the two elders, Hennen and Maybin, found themselves in the condition of seceders who were houseless in the streets. Fortunately a spiritual guide was immediately provided. The Rev. Joel Parker, in the service of the American Home Mission Society, being in the city, was at once solicited to become their stated supply. His connection began January 12, 1833, and the little band worshiped alternately with the organization formed a year before under Mr. Harris, in the wareroom on Lafayette square. These two wings finally coalesced in 1835. In March, 1834, Dr. Parker was unanimously chosen pastor, and on April 27th, was duly installed by the Presbytery of Mississippi. During this summer he was absent at the North, collecting funds for building a new house of worship. Some statements made by him to Northern audiences respecting the religious condition and necessities of New Orleans were grossly misrepresented in the public prints. A violent excitement was created against him in the city, indignation meetings were held, and he was once or twice burnt in effigy by the population. The storm was met with great firmness and dignity by the church, which rallied around its pastor, produced written evidence that Dr. Parker had been entirely misrepresented, and contended earnestly for the exercise of their own religious rights. In a short time, the fierce opposition was quelled, and was eventually lived down.

Upon the pastor's return in the autumn, worship was resumed in a room on Julia street until March 15, 1835, when the basement of the new building on Lafayette square was first occupied. This edifice, so well remembered by many present, was erected at an original cost, including the site, of $57,616. Subsequent improvements and enlargements, in 1844, with an additional purchase of ground, amounted to over $17,000 more; making the whole cost of the church, which was destroyed by fire in 1854, $75,000.

Dr. Parker's connection with the church extended over a period of five years and six months, from January 12, 1833, to June 14, 1838, at which date he left, never to return. The pastoral relation was not, however, dissolved till the spring of 1839. During his pastorship, the church was greatly prospered, having secured a commodious sanctuary, and showing, as early as 1836, a church-roll numbering one hundred and forty-two communicants. There were two elections of elders; in 1834, Dr. John R. Moore, Frederic R. Southmayd, and Truman Parmele being chosen to that office; and in 1838, Stephen Franklin, John S. Walton, and James Beattie.

The next incumbent of the pulpit was the Rev. Dr. John Breckinridge, with whom the church opened negotiations in February, 1839. This gentleman was at the time the Secretary of the Assembly's Board of Foreign Missions. In his letter to the church, dated May, 1839, he consents to serve it in conjunction with his secretaryship, from which his brethren were unwilling to release him, the Board giving him a dispensation for six or seven months for this purpose. These conditions being accepted, Dr. Breckinridge spent the winter of 1839 in New Orleans; and still again the winter of 1840, till April of 1841. He was called to the eternal rest in August, 1841, retaining in his hand the call of this church, as pastor elect. His labors were fragmentary, but efficient; and the church was left to mourn over hopes disappointed in his death.

The attention of the church was soon turned to the Rev. Dr. W. A. Scott, of Tuscaloosa, Alabama, who was installed as pastor on March 19, 1843, and whose pastoral relation was formally dissolved in September, 1855. His active connection with the church, however, began and closed earlier than these dates. His term of service, as pastor elect, began in the fall of 1842, and his active labors ceased in November, 1854, covering a period of twelve years. Dr. Scott's ministry was exceedingly productive, during which vigorous and constant efforts were made to build up the interests of Presbyterianism in the city. These will be briefly sketched in the notices soon to be given of the other church organizations. The roll of communicants swelled, in 1844, to four hundred and thirty-nine, and before the close of his ministry to over six hundred.

On July 20, 1845, Dr. J. M. W. Picton, and Charles Gardiner were ordained to the office of ruling elder; and Thomas Bowman and William P. Campbell, to that of deacon. On December 23, 1849, R. B. Shepherd, W. P. Campbell, and W. A. Bartlett were ordained to the eldership; and W. H. Reese, L. L. Brown, and James

Rainey, to the diaconate; and on November 28, 1852, the bench of deacons was increased by the installation of W. C. Black, Robert A. Grinnan, and Simon Devisser, and of J. G. Dunlap, on January 23, 1853.

The church edifice was burnt on October 29, 1854; and it is to the last degree creditable to the congregation that amidst all the discouragements of a vacant bishopric and a congregation scattered, it should have proceeded at once to build another of larger proportions and more finished in style. In 1857, the house in which we are now assembled was finished and dedicated to the worship of God. Its cost, with all its appointments, was about $87,000.

On September 21, 1854, a call was made out to the Rev. B. M. Palmer, of South Carolina, which, upon being presented before his Presbytery and Synod, was defeated by the refusal of those bodies to place it in his hands. The call was renewed on March 16, 1856, and prevailed. His labors began early in December of that year, and on the 28th of the same month he was installed by the Presbytery of New Orleans. After the lapse of seventeen years, he is present to-night to read this record of God's exceeding faithfulness and mercy to His redeemed people. It is only proper to add, that the membership of this church, which, after Dr. Scott's withdrawal, was thrown down to three hundred and fifty, was carried up in 1861, just before the war, to five hundred and thirty-one. By the war, in 1866, it was again reduced to four hundred and thirty-six, and now reaches to six hundred and forty-eight.

Three successful Mission schools are sustained and two buildings erected for their accommodation, one of these large and comfortable, at a cost of some $10,000. It is now sustaining a city missionary, which it has often done in the past, and always with marked results in the extension of the cause so dear to all our hearts.

We have preferred to give the history of this particular church without breaking its continuity. It is time, however, that we turn to the efforts of church extension, which will bring into view the other Presbyterian organizations in the city.

The first effort in this direction was the employment, on January 30, 1840, by the Session of the First Church, of Rev. Jerome Twichell, as a city missionary, with four points of labor, viz.: in the lecture-room, to the colored people; at Orleans Cotton Press to the seamen; at the city prison, and in the District of Lafayette. Mr. Twichell began his work at once, opening a service in the house of Mrs. Dick, on February 4—thirty persons being present. This was the germ of the Lafayette Presbyterian Church, now under the pastoral care of Rev. Dr. Markham. On March 1, divine service was transferred to the Lafayette Court-room. On March 19, a meeting was held of the citizens of the district, to consider the erection of a church-edifice, which was prosecuted with such vigor, that in January, 1842, a house of worship was finished, at a cost of some $5,000, and dedicated, on Fulton street, between Josephine and St. Andrew.

The Lafayette Church was not, however, organized till September 21, 1843, when twenty members of the First Church were set off as a colony for this purpose, Dr. John Rollins, Richard Leech, and John Hume being the first elders.

Rev. Jerome Twichell was elected pastor and installed, the first Sabbath in January, 1844, and continued in this relation till December 4, 1853—ten years.

His successor, Rev. J. Sidney Hays, was installed May 7, 1854, who died of yellow fever, August 26, 1855, having served one year and four months. Sixteen months elapsed before the sad vacancy was filled. On February 1, 1857, Rev. T. R. Markham, then a licentiate, was engaged as a supply for one year; on May 24 he was ordained as an evangelist; elected pastor, December 20, and installed on January 24, 1858. His efficient ministry continues to the present time, covering a period of more than sixteen years.

On Sabbath night, November 18, 1860, the church building was destroyed by fire, and the congregation assembled for worship in Union Hall on Jackson street, until the Federal occupation of the city, May, 1862. After the war, the church held its services in the First German Church on First street until April, 1867, when they entered their present comfortable and handsome building on Magazine street, above Jackson, which was dedicated on the following Sabbath, April 14. The cost of this structure, with ground, is about $45,000.

The growth of this church, the first off-shoot from the parent church, was, at first, gradual and slow. In 1844, the membership is reported to be twenty-three. In 1855, it had increased only to thirty-seven. In 1858, to fifty. In 1866, the first year after the war, the church-roll presents one hundred and thirty communicants, and in 1873, this number has increased to four hundred and thirty-five.

The next enterprise undertaken resulted in the organization of what was known as the *Second Church*, at the corner of Prytania and Calliope streets, which is now extinct, the building having passed into the hands of another denomination. It appears from the minutes of the First Church, that on November 13, 1843, the Rev. R. L. Stanton, of Woodville, accepted an invitation to serve as a city missionary, and in April, 1845, twenty-two persons were set off as a nucleus to form the Second

Church, under Mr. Stanton, whose relations as a missionary under Session of First Church ceased about May 15 of the same year. Lots were purchased in 1844 on the corner of Prytania and Calliope streets, and a church building erected. Mr. Stanton resigned about 1852, to assume the presidency of Oakland College; and in 1853 his place was supplied by Rev. Dr. S. Woodbridge, who died in 1863. The enterprise was never a successful one, due, we think, in part to its location, which, after the inauguration of the Prytania Street Church, was something like a trough of the sea, between it and the First Church. After the war, the church was dissolved by act of Presbytery, its roll being transferred to the Thalia Street Church, except in cases where the members preferred to attach themselves elsewhere.

The next enterprise undertaken laid the foundation of what is known as the *Third Church.* In the autumn of 1844, a few members of the First Church established a Sabbath school in the Third district, under the superintendency of Mr. F. Stringer. The ground floor of No. 20 Moreau street was fitted up, and divine service conducted by Rev. E. R. Beadle, for about six months. The school was then removed to Mr. Elkin's house on Chartres street. In the fall of 1845, Rev. James Beattie took charge of the mission, and opened service in his own house on Esplanade street, near Burgundy. On March 7, 1847, after a sermon by Rev. Dr. W. A. Scott, the Third Church was organized with a colony of eighteen members set off from the First Church, F. Stringer and C. C. Lyon, elders, Mr. Beattie continuing in charge till 1850, when he removed with his family to the North.

In 1848, a neat frame building, with about one hundred and fifty sittings, was erected on Casacalvo street, at an expense of some $2,500, which was occupied by the congregation until the completion of its present large and tasteful house of worship on Washington square. This building was begun in 1858, and completed by January 1, 1860, at a cost of about $45,000.

In December, 1850, Rev. D. S. Baker succeeded Mr. Beattie in the pulpit, and continued till August, 1852. From that time till February, 1854, the church was without a regular supply, when Rev. James Richards became its pastor, which relation was terminated in March, 1855, about one year. From that time to January, 1857, the church was served by Rev. N. G. North, at which date begins the term of its present pastor, the Rev. Dr. H. M. Smith, lasting now almost seventeen years.

In 1850 the church reported a membership of forty-four; in 1855, a membership of forty-two; in 1857, a membership of fifty-three; in 1860, a membership of seventy-one; and now, of one hundred and two. F. Stringer and W. C. Raymond, elders.

The growth of this church is impaired by the constant tendency of English-speaking residents to move above Canal street.

These three churches were directly colonized from the First Church. The Prytania Street organization was an independent movement, originating nearly at the same time and in the same way with the Third Church. A mission Sabbath school was started up town. In 1846, three lots were purchased for $1,285, at the corner of Prytania and Josephine streets, and a small frame building erected at a cost of $1,342, which has since been enlarged into their present lecture room. The Rev. E. R. Beadle, brought here by the First Church as a city missionary in conjunction with the editorship of the *New Orleans Protestant*, was identified with the movement from the beginning. On May 31, 1846, the church was organized by the Presbytery of Louisiana, with twelve members, six male and six female; of whom three were from the First Church, two from the Second, and seven from the Fulton Street, now the Lafayette Church. Mr. David Hadden was the first elder, and H. T. Bartlett the first deacon. In June, Mr. Beadle was chosen pastor, who served six years, until September, 1852. During his term, the present church building was erected, in the winters of 1848–9, at a cost of $14,040; and the membership was increased from twelve to one hundred and thirty.

The second pastor, Rev. Isaac Henderson, was called in November, 1852, and served till April, 1865, a period of twelve years and six months. During an interval of twenty months, the pulpit was supplied by the Rev. B. Wayne and Rev. W. F. V. Barlett, till December 9, 1866, when Rev. R. Q. Mallard, the present pastor, was installed.

The increase of its communicants is as follows: At its organization, in 1846, twelve; on September 21, 1852, one hundred and thirty; on April 2, 1855, two hundred and eleven; on March 30, 1857, one hundred and ninety-eight; on December 9, 1866, when present pastorship began, one hundred and fifty-seven; at the present time, two hundred and twenty-eight.

In January, 1854, a colony of seventeen Germans, gathered in by Mr. Young, as colporteur, was set off to form the First German Church, which, though now in connection with the Northern Assembly, is the direct fruit of missionary labor by Presbyterians in this city.

In 1860, also, a colony of twelve was set off, with Mr. H. T. Bartlett at its head, to reinforce the Thalia Street Church. It now maintains a flourishing mission Sabbath school, and has erected a suitable building for the same.

Through the agency of a general committee of domestic missions, chapels were erected on Canal street, corner of Franklin; on Thalia street, corner of Franklin; in Jefferson City, and in Carrollton. Their cost cannot well be ascertained, the records of this committee having been lost. The property in each case has been conveyed to the congregations worshiping therein, as soon as incorporated.

As early as 1845, Rev. Noah F. Packard preached in the Canal Street Chapel, and died of yellow fever in 1846. On April 11, 1847, a church was organized by the Presbytery of Louisiana, known as the *Fourth Church*, with nine members, of whom five were from the First Church, and four were from abroad. Heman Packard was the first elder, and Alexander Reid the first deacon.

On March 1, 1848, a call was made to Rev. Henry G. Blinn, a licentiate, which was renewed November 27 of the same year, from which moment his name disappears from the record.

On March 12, 1854, Rev. William McConnell was chosen pastor, the membership being twenty-five, which soon increased to fifty-two, and in 1857 to sixty-nine; Viall, Young, and Henderson being added to the eldership.

Rev. Gaylord L. Moore succeeded Mr. McConnell as pastor from 1858 to May, 1863. During his administration a new and large church was built, at a cost of over $40,000, on the corner of Gasquet and Liberty streets, the basement of which was occupied in May, 1860, and the church itself dedicated in November of the same year. Mr. Moore returned in the autumn of 1865, after the war, and remained in charge of the pulpit till June, 1868. He was succeeded in December of that year by Rev. A. F. Dickson, whose term of service continued three years. Under a financial pressure, the church building was sold in May, 1871, and a better location purchased, and a new but smaller building erected, at the corner of Canal and Derbigny streets. The enterprise is now free from debt, and only needs a faithful pastor in order to spring forth upon a more hopeful career. Its present membership is one hundred and thirty-five.

An attempt to organize a church in the Thalia Chapel was made by Rev. N. G. North, as early as January 16, 1853, with seventeen members. The organization was not completed by the election of elders, and appears to have lapsed. An irregular mission was maintained, principally through a Sabbath school, till June, 1860; when a church was fully organized by the Presbytery with twelve members set off from Prytania Street congregation, and two additional on profession. H. T. Bartlett and A. D. Donovan were the first elders; A. E. Gillett, F. Beaumont, and J. A. Hall, the first deacons.

The infant church was served by Rev. Dr. Wm. Fisher, from November, 1860, to May 30, 1861. On October 27, 1861, Rev. W. A. Hall was called to the pastorate, and resigned October 25, 1866, five years. On December 12, 1867, Rev. W. C. Dunlap became the supply, and closed his connection, October 4, 1868. On February 5, 1869, Rev. Wm. Flinn was chosen pastor, and was installed in the April following. During this pastorate, which still happily continues, one hundred and six have been added to the church membership, of whom seventy-three have been received on profession of faith. The congregation has built a comfortable parsonage, and hopes soon to erect a new house of worship, corner of Franklin and Euterpe streets, for which it has funds in bank between $15,000 and $16,000, and for which its present property will be further available.

In the Bouligny chapel, built 1850, an irregular mission was conducted with varying success, till 1860, when regular preaching was begun there by Rev. B. Wayne. In May, 1861, a church was organized by the Presbytery of New Orleans, now known as the Napoleon Avenue Church, with twenty members, John Dyer, the only elder. The war came on, and everything was suspended; on the return of peace, services were resumed, and have since been regularly maintained. In March, 1870, the present location on Napoleon avenue was purchased; in December, 1871, a new brick building was commenced, and sufficiently finished in July, 1872, to be occupied, in a rude and incomplete condition. During the past season it has been entirely finished, and in September, 1873, was publicly dedicated, free of debt, to the worship of Almighty God. This handsome structure, with all its appointments, and with the ground on which it stands, has cost the sum of $18,000, a monument to the liberality of our people, and to the enterprise and zeal of the pastor and congregation who have persistently carried it through. Chiefly since the war, one hundred and forty-eight persons have been received into its membership, of whom one hundred and eleven were on profession of faith. The present roll numbers seventy members. Messrs. G. W. H. Marr and S. McGinnis are the elders.

On September 1, 1855, a church was organized by the Presbytery, at Carrollton, with seventeen members, of whom seven were from the First Church, nine from the Prytania Street Church, and one from the Second Church; J. S. McComb, H. T. Bartlett, and R. G. Latting were chosen elders. On February 4, 1856, Rev. N. P. Chamberlain was chosen pastor, and served in this relation till January 31, 1858, a period of two years. The pulpit was kept open by supplies, principally Rev.

Dr. J. R. Hutchison, Principal of Belle Grove Collegiate Institute, till everything was broken up by the war, and Dr. Hutchison removed to Houston. In 1866, it appearing that the church had been so reduced that there were no elders, and not even a male member, Carrollton was taken under care of the Presbytery as a Mission station, and is at present held as such against a better time for re-organization. It enjoys the efficient labors of Elder Joseph A. Maybin, which have been greatly blessed, and yield promise that the church may at no distant day be revived.

In this roll of our churches must be added the *Second German Church*, organized during the war; with its pastor, Rev. F. O. Koelle, and a membership of fifty-six, it is now in full connection with the Presbytery of New Orleans. Its handsome and commodious house of worship is on lower Claiborne street.

The limits within which we are restrained will not suffer any mention to be made of the efforts to establish a religious newspaper, and also a Depository; except to say, that after innumerable backsets, they have both proved successful; the Synod of Mississippi being in possession of a valuable property in its Depository building, and also of an able and influential paper, edited by the Rev. Dr. Smith.

From this meager sketch, we may gather some impression of the growth of Presbyterianism in this city. In 1818, it started from nothing; in 1823, the church re-organized with twenty-four members. Ten years later it found itself thrown back upon this identical number, and was forced to begin anew in the midst of feuds and dissensions, and with its good name discredited before the world. Our real progress dates from 1833, starting with twenty-four; to-day, after the lapse of forty years, we count *nine* organized churches, including the

First German; which, though it has bolted, and is now under the jurisdiction of the Northern Assembly, is nevertheless a part of this historical development and a fruit of missionary zeal put forth by ourselves. In addition, there are two or three hopeful Mission stations, where the experience of the past justifies the expectation that they will eventually crystallize into churches. Our original number of twenty-three has increased nearly to two thousand communicants; and with about two thousand three hundred children in our various Sabbath schools. "Though our beginning was small, yet our latter end hath greatly increased." We may truly say with the Patriarch Jacob, "with my staff I passed over this Jordan, and now I am become two bands." Surely on this Fiftieth Anniversary, we may exclaim, looking back over the past, "What hath God wrought!" With our present point of support, and the immense leverage we have thereby gained, what may not be accomplished during the fifty years which are to come! May God give to us, and to those who shall succeed us, grace to fulfill the precious and solemn trust; that when the Century of Presbyterianism shall be observed here, "the handful of corn," sown by our fathers "upon the top of the mountain," may be seen in "its fruit to shake like Lebanon"—and "they of the city to flourish like grass of the earth!"

Rev. Wm. Flinn read the Hymn,

"Glorious things of thee are spoken,
Zion, City of our God,"

and the congregation rose and sang.

REMINISCENCES.

The venerable Joseph A. Maybin, for forty-five years a ruling elder, and the oldest surviving member of this church, followed, with interesting personal reminiscences, beginning with Larned's arrival in the city, January 22, 1818.

The following is a synopsis.

At that time there was little of the city this side of Canal street. There was then only one Protestant church below Canal, and that was Episcopal, situated on the corner of Bourbon and Canal streets.

Sylvester Larned, the first Presbyterian minister, arrived in this city about the time that the present minister of the First Presbyterian Church was born. The Rev. Mr. Hull, the Episcopal minister, generously permitted the use of his church to the Presbyterians from one until four in the afternoon, at which hours Mr. Larned would preach. His eloquence soon attracted attention, and an effort was made to erect a Presbyterian place of worship. Some were of the opinion that New Orleans could not support two Protestant places of worship—the city was too small for that—yet, notwithstanding, the Presbyterians were successful in obtaining a place of worship on the site of the building now occupied by Stauffer, Macready & Co., on Canal street.

Mr. Larned attended the Presbytery of Mississippi the year before his death. While there, the yellow fever broke out in the city, and he was advised, by his trustees and the physicians, not to return to New Orleans until the danger had passed. To this he consented reluctantly; and his sensitive spirit, being galled by the reproach that he had fled from the fever, the next year he stood at his post like the brave man that he was. His sense of honor would not allow him to leave, and he remained in New Orleans to die. From the little one-story building on Camp street, nearly opposite the upper corner of Lafayette square, within a square of this church, all that remained of Sylvester Larned was conveyed to the Girod street cemetery.

He was a man of strong social feelings, peculiarly adapted to please the Southern people. He had a heart "broad as the heavens and deep as the ocean." His brow was open, his eye gentle, features intellectual; in person reminding you of the Apollo Belvidere; of a sweet and affectionate disposition, and a "silver-tongued voice" that rolled music, and captivated all his hearers. Said a distinguished judge once of him, "I cannot go to hear that young man because he makes me shed tears."

Mr. Clapp was a great conversationalist. His style of delivery was impressive and eloquent. His mind was neither analytical nor logical, still less, profound. He impressed his audience and had many warm personal friends, whom he retained even after he left this city, and who generously contributed to his support until his death at Louisville in 1866.

The Rev. Mr. Parker, who followed Mr. Clapp, walked from his home in Vermont to Union College at Schenectady, New York. He represented to the professors that his father was a poor farmer and a revolutionary soldier, that he could not afford to furnish the money required for his education, but that if they would give him work, he would try and repay them for the trouble and expense of his graduation. The professors were pleased with his determination, and Parker studied for the ministry. He was a man of great decision of character, vigorous and logical, plain in person, not prepossessing in feature, and not calculated to obtain and keep personal friends. Yet he was a man spoken of as having the highest order of talent as a minister of the Gospel.

In the summer of 1834 he was sent North to solicit subscriptions in the larger cities, for the purpose of obtaining, if possible, a sum sufficient to finish the church then building. While on the tour it was represented that he had stated "that there were forty thousand Catholics in the city of New Orleans who were atheists, and that the Protestants were no better." This statement was published in the newspapers and copied into the *New Orleans Bulletin*, creating great excitement and indignation. Mr. Parker replied to the charges made in one of the newspapers North, denying that he had made any such statement. The Mayor of this city advised that "that priest" be sent away, and—if Mr. Maybin was not mistaken—a proclamation was issued commanding the peace. When it was known that he was returning to this city word was sent to the Balize that he be landed before the arrival of the packet in New Orleans, and Mr. Parker was accordingly put off at the English turn. The next day he arrived in New Orleans, and appeared upon the streets to vindicate his innocence. A meeting was called the next day at the City Hotel, at which Mr. Parker was requested to explain. He made a clear statement, but the people were not satisfied. Resolutions were drawn up and passed, that he leave the city, that the elders of the church dismiss him, etc. A meeting of the members of the church was immediately called. Fifty attended. They one and all supported Mr. Parker as being in the right. They all believed his representation made at the City Hotel, and declared they had a right to have for a pastor whom they pleased, and they intended to maintain that right; and they did, and Mr. Parker was retained. That was a trying hour in the history of the Protestant Church in this city, but the storm was weathered. If Mr. Parker was abandoned, what security had other pastors that they would be retained. They were weak, feeble, discouraged, but they stood their ground and conquered. Like the weak little band of Apostles on the sea of Galilee when they called upon the Saviour to stay the storm, while the waves ran mountain high and threatened to dash their little bark to pieces, the storm was hushed by the Master. He said to the waves "be still," and they went down. He bade the winds to cease, and they slept as gently as a babe upon the bosom of its mother.

Rev. Dr. John Breckinridge, descended from the pioneer stock of Kentucky heroes, was the next pastor. A courteous and polished gentleman, with a sweet voice and a flow of native eloquence, but a feeble frame; his brief pastorate was soon closed by death. His successor was Rev. W. A. Scott, who at the age of eighteen, entered the army as Chaplain, by appointment from President Jackson, and was thus enabled to save sufficient money to finish his theological education at Princeton.

Mr. Scott was called to this position from the pastoral charge of the church at Tuscaloosa, Ala., his Presbytery, as in the case of the present pastor, having at first refused to place the call in his hands. Dr. Scott was an attractive and eloquent preacher, distinguished for his ability to set forth the truth by illustrations drawn from all sources, whether from nature or the customs and institutions of men.

In referring to those who rendered most effective co-operation in building up Presbyterianism in New Orleans he paid a passing tribute to the late Nathan Goodale, elder of the Lafayette Church—"whose every vein was filled with philanthropy." All honor to the little band of twenty-four, who comprised the original church organization—would you see their monument—look around upon this congregation! "Are they not at this moment, while singing their songs of everlasting praise—looking down on this scene from Heaven?"

You see before you the last elder of that band—standing as an isthmus between the present and the past, the last connecting link. It is to me a crushing thought.

On this occasion, and it may be my last opportunity, I desire to return my humble and heartfelt thanks to the pastor, elders, and members of this church for all the kindness I have ever received at their hands.

And now I want to declare that it is my wish to die in the service of this honored church; and that my children and children's children may die in the same faith. I stand here—a brand snatched from the burning. And when I die let it be inscribed on my coffin over my heart, "It is a faithful saying and worthy of all acceptation, that Jesus Christ came into the world to save sinners, of whom I—I—I—am chief!"

The congregation then sang,

"I love thy Kingdom, Lord."

Dr. Smith then read the following historical paper:

THE ORIGIN AND GROWTH OF PRESBYTERIANISM IN THE SOUTHWEST.

The history of our Church in New Orleans, belongs to the history of the Church in the Southwest. We shall better appreciate the significance of the chapter which concludes our work, if we glance at the more general movement of which it forms such an important part. To do this, we must go back into the past more than a quarter of a century before our work in the city was organized; even to the times when the tide of our immigration was first turned in this direction.

The settlement of the Southwest was much encouraged by the policy of the British Government. At the close of the French war of 1763, she obtained the

Natchez country and East and West Florida. West Florida was attached to the Natchez country, and settlers were attracted by liberal grants of land.

One result—unfortunately—of our war of the Revolution was, that this country was ceded back to Spain. The Natchez country thus became a Spanish Province, and continued to be for twenty years. By the Spanish authorities Protestant worship was decreed to be a criminal offense. Intolerant laws were enacted and remorselessly enforced. Three quarters of a century ago Presbyterians at Natchez could not worship God without a sentinel at the door to warn them of danger. Persons detected in this crime were arrested, thrown into a filthy prison until they gave bonds not to repeat the offense, and were threatened if detected in repeating this offense to be sent to the mines of Mexico. Many were imprisoned. Among those imprisoned for holding prayer-meetings was John Bolls, a ruling elder of the Presbyterian Church, from North Carolina, who had served in the Revolutionary war.

John Bolls was not destined to slavery in the mines of Mexico, for this distressing state of things at length came to an end. On the night of March 29, 1798, the Spanish commandant evacuated the post. Next morning the American flag floated from the walls of Fort St. Rosalie, and religious liberty found shelter beneath its folds.

It would be hard to enumerate the various routes by which you may gain access to the Southwest now, but in the year A. D. 1800, the best known land route was a bridle path. The Natchez trace was an Indian trail from Nashville, which could be traveled only on horseback or on foot. It passed through tangled forests and swamps, through warlike Indian tribes, and was infested by bands of lawless desperadoes, more dreaded than the

Indians themselves. Along this friendless path came Hall, Montgomery, and Bowman, missionaries sent from the Synod of the Carolinas. Amidst the perils of this adventurous journey they found, at Pontotoc, Joseph Bullen, missionary to the Indians, sent there by the New York Missionary Society in 1797, and after meeting this sympathizing laborer they entered again on their perilous journey, evaded death and outstripped starvation, and, finally, reached Natchez, the field of their future labors. These were the pioneers of our Church in the Southwest.

At that time there were about seven thousand Americans in the province. From many of these the missionaries met a cordial reception. With Natchez as their headquarters, they entered on their work, and visited the settlements, and established preaching places; gathering up the scattered Presbyterians and forming them into communities, soon to grow up into organized churches. In a year or two they returned home. But Joseph Bullen, the Indian missionary, took up the work they had begun. Coming southward in 1803, he preached with great acceptability to these congregations. And in A. D. 1804, it was his privilege to organize the first Presbyterian church established in the Southwest. It was well named Bethel. It has survived, too, the many changes that have intervened, and is existing still.

For years afterwards, the Synod of the Carolinas continued to send missionaries to this field, and other churches were organized from time to time. At length the need of Presbyterial jurisdiction came to be felt. At that time the general jurisdiction of this region was vested in the Synod of Kentucky. Ten years after the first church was organized, the Synod of Kentucky was overtured to establish the *Presbytery of Mississippi*, which was done A. D. 1815. And the name of John

Bolls stands first on the list of its ruling elders, as the representative of the first church organized in the Southwest.

In the year 1818, the honored name of Sylvester Larned was added to the list of its members. And in 1823 the Presbyterian Church in New Orleans was placed upon its roll, and two important streams of influence coalesced, to form thereafter but one current of moral energy.

The *Presbytery of Mississippi,* when organized, formed part of the Synod of Kentucky. The movement of population, and the expansion of our church, involved certain changes in its subsequent relations. In 1817, it was associated with the Synod of Tennessee. In 1826, we find it placed upon the roll of the Synod of West Tennessee. But in 1829, in connection with other Presbyteries, which appear to have been set off from its territory, it was erected into a Synod, called the *Synod of Mississippi and South Alabama.* In 1835, three Presbyteries were set off from this growing Synod to form the *Synod of Alabama,* and from that time it is known as the *Synod of Mississippi.* God so prospered this Synod, that in 1847 it became necessary to divide it again, and four more Presbyteries were set off to form the *Synod of Memphis.* And in 1851, three more of its Presbyteries were erected into the *Synod of Texas.* And in 1852, out of the territory ceded to the Synod of Memphis, there was formed still another Synod, the *Synod of Arkansas.*

In the light of this interesting record, the unity of sentiment and harmony of purpose which have hitherto prevailed among us in the Southwest, cannot seem surprising. Our membership is largely drawn by descent from the Presbyterian stock of the best of the older communities; bound together by strong ecclesiastical family-ties; linked together in common interests, and laboring shoulder to shoulder in a common cause; we constitute, to a large extent, a homogeneous Presbyterianism, whose moral influence, if combined and wisely directed, must prove a permanent benefit to the world.

The piety of those formative times was bold and aggressive. For many years, while the country as yet was new, camp-meetings were annually held at some central point, easy of access to a wide region of country. To these points people from long distances would come, to spend a week or two in waiting on God, and seeking his face. Immense assemblies would congregate in these cathedrals of the wilderness, and great religious revivals were often the result. The utmost decorum prevailed on such occasions, and unbounded hospitality made all comers welcome. It was not unusual for the Presbyteries to convene at these meetings. And on one occasion, as we told, a meeting of the Synod was held.

The style of doing the work of the Gospel was adapted to the needs of the times. And the work was blessed. These meetings were not discontinued until facilities for public worship became more abundant, when the necessity for them had accordingly passed away.

The spirit of the Synod, also, was a missionary spirit. With such men as Montgomery, Smylie, Kingsbury, Alfred Wright, Moore, and Chase, men of apostolic zeal, amongst its members, it could not be otherwise. Such men prosecuted their missionary work under its jurisdiction. After the manner of the Synod of the Carolinas, it sent out its evangelists into the broad domain of Texas, as soon as the Republic was established. And we find it overturing the Assembly to consider the question of sending missionaries to Mexico and Oregon. It never shrunk from the call to press the evangelistic work in any direction. So that, in the course of time, there has passed under its jurisdiction a territory which stretches from Georgia to the Rio Grande, and which reaches northward far enough to include the State of Arkansas, and the Indian nation.

Texas will have a religious history of its own, and it will be characteristic, as it ought to be. It will be found that it was born in battle—the offspring of that struggle for constitutional liberty which planted Travis, Bonham, and Crockett, with their little band of heroes, in the path of the ferocious army of Santa Anna. The massacre of the Alamo, in 1836, was undoubtedly the Thermopylæ of civil and religious liberty for the far Southwest.

That form of Christianity will best succeed among its diversified and scattered communities which most clearly enunciates the simple principles of the Gospel, and best illustrates the power of vital godliness. In these respects, it seems to us, our Church in that State has a great work before it. So we find one little band borrowing the use of a blacksmith's shop to inaugurate public worship, then and there laying the foundations of an important and influential church. Elsewhere we see some Scotch-Irish elder assembling his neighbors in his house for prayer-meetings, and laying the foundations of another church. And again, we find the unconverted son of pious parents appalled by the surrounding destitutions, feeling that the responsibility for the continuance of this spiritual ignorance rests on his own conscience, essaying to meet it by establishing Sabbath-schools and Bible-classes; and carrying them on, to the best of his ability, until such time as it may please God to relieve him from the duty, which God so mysteriously laid upon him. In so far as our people courageously accept these allotments of Providence, they represent a form of Christianity full of vital force and growth, and set forth, by pure principles and a consistent, earnest activity, that blessed Gospel which in all possible emergencies is the one thing needful for man. No one can tell how much, and in how many instances, the Gospel has been, and still is, proclaimed in our sister State through such unpretending but noble instruments. The coming years will rejoice in the harvest, but the names of those who planted for it, it must be left for eternity to disclose.

It becomes us, also, to refer with gratitude to the results of our work, as a Church, among the Indian tribes of the Southwest. It is a much greater work than is generally known. There is far more piety and Christian character, and a far greater knowledge and appreciation of Christian truth, among the tribes brought into contact with the institutions of Christianity than is believed by the uninformed. In the bounds of the Creek nation, the Baptists report twenty-four ordained Indian preachers, some of whom are well known Creek and Seminole chiefs. The Methodist Church South can claim a similar record. From the times of Joseph Bullen, the Indian missionary and founder of the First Presbyterian Church in the Southwest, until to-day, our church has evinced a deep and constant interest in the welfare of those tribes. Perhaps the most important mission work among them is conducted by the Southern Presbyterian Church. And what is the result of these various labors? It is this. They have printing-presses, newspapers, and books; they have preachers of their own race—men of culture, piety, and moral power; and, in proportion to their population, the people of the Indian nation have more schools, more churches, attend more largely religious worship, and contribute more money for religious purposes than the people of any Territory in the United States.

It is a strange mistake to suppose that the nature of the Indian cannot be brought under the power of the principles of the Gospel. At a Bible Anniversary in one of our Western cities not long since, one of those Indian chiefs stepped forward, and with intense feeling, said, "When I come from among my people and visit the cities, I hear white men debating, whether it is of any use to send the Gospel to the heathen? Some seem to think that it is of no use; that the Gospel cannot convert the heathen. *It is of use* to send the Gospel to the heathen. I and my people were heathen; we believed in all its silly and degrading superstitions; we worshiped we knew not what; we knew of no future for the soul; we were without God and without hope. But now the true light shines among us. We know and love God, and we live in hope of a happy home beyond the grave. This is what the Gospel has done for us. Let no man doubt that the Gospel has power to convert the heathen! I was a heathen, and it converted me."

Who shall gainsay such testimony to the work which it has pleased God to accomplish, by those who have preceded us in this field?

Our Church in the Southwest may not boast of having achieved all that it aimed to achieve. Perhaps a sense of comparative failure and shortcoming has attended its most successful enterprises. Nevertheless, there is much to gratify a Christian heart in the contrast between its present efficiency and its humble origin. There is no great interval between the extensive religious liberty and influence which we enjoy to-day, and that Spanish prison at Natchez—and the connection is not hard to trace. It is only another illustration of God's fidelity in rewarding the devotedness of his servants. John Bolls' prayer-meeting led him to a Spanish prison seventy-five years ago; and slavery in the mines of Mexico seemed to be the inevitable result of them. But where duty to God is concerned, the apparent result is often vastly different from the actual result. Could he have looked through the bars of his prison on the field of religious activity, of which that prison was destined to be the center—could his eye have pierced the veil of three-quarters of a century, he would have seen this wide territory covered with a goodly family of five Synods, twenty Presbyteries, and nearly six hundred churches; together with all the multiform kinds of moral, benevolent, and religious enterprises which they represent or sustain.

The history of the world does not often produce, in such a limited period, and from such a despised beginning, a more glorious result.

Yet this was not merely the work of one man, nor is it the mere development of any one line or form of effort. Many a worker wrought in that field—each in his own sphere, at his own work, in his own way—known or unknown, scattered or united, organized or unorganized —but each and all for the Lord. And by the mysterious control of an Almighty hand, all things, whether good or evil, or the work of friend or foe, were ruled and overruled, and made to combine and co-operate to accomplish his gracious purpose.

The future may have great things in store for us, but it can teach us no better than the past has taught us, that great lesson that fidelity to God is not lost—neither is it to be held as of little moment, though it be obscure and seemingly uninfluential. However trivial it may seem, each particular and individual movement must live till it obeys the laws of a divine attraction, and combines with a greater, which shall lead it on till it co-operate even with the greatest.

We may be as insignificant as the raindrop on the

mountain side; yet that drop must not perish till it blends with others, and compels the rivulet to spring into being. And the rivulets can find no rest, until they make to bound forth into life the growing river, wealth-bearing and life-producing. Nor can the rivers return or cease, till they have mingled their mighty burdens on the bosom of the deep. And so the act of fidelity and the prayer of faith; the godly life and the preached word; prayer-meetings and Sunday-schools will join and conjoin, and operate and co-operate, increase and multiply, overleap all restraints, and in their ebb and flow bear down and continue to bear down all opposing forces. Out of the feeble will come the strong, and from the bosom of patience shall leap forth might; till the grace of God shall sweep over society like the tides of the ocean in their strength; till the knowledge of God shall fill and cover the earth; till the time shall come, when rejoicing angels shall declare, "It is finished," "The kingdoms of this world have become the empire of our God."

Dr. T. R. Markham, and Rev. R. Q. Mallard delivered addresses admirably illustrating the aggressive movement of the Church, through the two arms of her service, the pastorship, and the pulpit; the one urging home the Gospel to the heart of the individual, in personal intercourse; the other, in the stated systematic presentation of truth to the masses.

The audience then rose and sung

"All hail the power of Jesus' name."

The benediction was then pronounced by Rev. W. Flinn.

TEXAS.

If you look at the map, you will see that the Gulf of Mexico is somewhat in the shape of a horse-shoe. Its opening is defended and adorned by the island of Cuba. Commencing at Cape Florida, we find that its capes and harbors are very numerous, and are sufficient for the vast commerce of this great inland sea, and the rich territories that border it. They are Tampa, Apalachee, Mobile, New Orleans, Atchafalaya, Calcasieu, Sabine, Galveston, Brazos River, Matagorda, Corpus Christi, Brazos Santiago, Tehuantepec, Campeachy, and Sisal.

At the toe of this great shoe lies the State of Texas, reaching for a distance of four hundred miles along the coast, and embracing in its entire boundaries two hundred and thirty-seven thousand square miles, or about one hundred and fifty millions of acres. It is four times as large as Virginia. The country along the coast is a level prairie; but as you pass to the interior, the surface gradually rises and becomes more uneven; and still further inland, it becomes hilly and mountainous. After crossing an extensive belt of timber, and reaching more than a hundred miles from the coast, you find the high rolling prairies, composed of the richest soil in the world, covered with musquit-grass, and having along the streams and valleys sufficient timber for all needful purposes.

Texas is what is called an alluvial country, and bears strong evidence of having been once under water. Very little rock is found, except in the northern part. It possesses every variety of climate and surface, and there is nothing which can contribute to the comfort and wants of man which will not grow here. Oranges and sugar-cane flourish in the south; cotton in the middle regions; wheat in the north; and potatoes, corn and vegetables flourish everywhere; while countless numbers of cattle, horses, sheep, and hogs can be reared in any part of the State. In fact, there is no country on the continent better suited to become the abode of millions of contented and happy people. It is a world in itself, where nature teems with all kind of riches, and holds out all kind of attractions to people of other States to come and find homes for themselves and their children. Our only wonder is, that so boundless a country has remained so long without being filled up with civilized people.

INDIANS IN TEXAS.

The Indians, from their mode of living, and the continual wars among their different tribes, were but thinly scattered over the immense country lying between the Rio Grande and Red River. The Lipans and the Carankaws lived along the lower Rio Grande and the Colorado and Brazos. They subsisted mainly upon fish. The next tribe, going east, was the Cenis, inhabiting Buffalo Bayou, the San Jacinto Valley, and the Trinity River. On the banks of the Trinity their villages were large and numerous. Their habitations were like bee-hives, and some of them were forty feet high. As they devoted much time to raising corn, they were comparatively wealthy. They traded with the Spaniards of New Mexico, from whom they procured horses, money, spurs, and clothing. The next tribe east were the Nassoriis, living between the Cenis and the Sabine River. These four tribes, two centuries ago, formed the original inhabitants of Texas. The landing of the colony of La Salle was to them a new and wonderful event. The sight of ships and the sound of fire-arms were to them subjects of awe and astonishment. Living in the simplicity of nature, they were free from most of the diseases and vices of European nations. They were worshipers of the sun, and full of the superstitions common to other North American Indians. They had their rain-makers, their game-finders, and their witches. Living in a mild climate, and among prairies covered with buffalo and game of all kinds, and near streams and bays abounding in fish, they obtained their living with but little effort. They were contented and as free as people ever can become who know nothing of the usages of civilized life.

Early and vigorous efforts were made by Catholic missionaries to convert them to Christianity. Establishments were formed called *presidios* or *missions.* Buildings were erected round a square, and consisted of a church, storehouses, dwellings for priests, officers, and soldiers. Huts were erected at a short distance for the converted Indians. The ruins of many of these old presidios remain to this day. But the Indians are now all gone, and none are found except on the northern and western frontiers of the State. One race has disappeared, and a new one is fast filling its place. The weak have yielded to the strong—the savage to the civilized; and before many years roll round, the only record of once powerful Indian tribes will be the beautiful names which still cling to some of our rivers and our mountains.

THE FRENCH IN TEXAS.

The first Europeans who visited Texas were led here by La Salle, who landed near the entrance of Matagorda Bay, on February 18, 1685. La Salle was a brave and gallant knight under Louis XIV., King of France. Born of a good family, and intended for the priesthood in the Catholic Church, he had received a finished education. He was a man of great talents, of an enterprising spirit, and possessed firmness of mind which danger and adversity seemed only to strengthen. He kept his own secrets, relied upon his own genius, and bore without a murmur whatever ills befell him.

A squadron of four vessels was provided and furnished by the king, and the whole number of persons embarked in the enterprise, was three hundred. The squadron first touched land near Sabine Bay, but making no discoveries, and being unable to get any information from the Indians, they proceeded westward, and sailing through Pass Cavallo, entered the Bay of St. Bernard, since known by its present name. One of the vessels was wrecked in attempting to land. The others landed in safety, and a camp was formed on the west side near the entrance of the Bay. The little colony was greatly refreshed by an abundance of game and fish. They were charmed with the country. The herds of buffalo and deer that were seen grazing on the prairies, the innumerable wild flowers that covered the earth, and the birds that warbled in the trees, led them to believe that they had found an earthly paradise.

But these bright prospects were soon clouded. Troubles arose with the Indians. Their chief supply of provisions was lost. Sickness began to thin their numbers. Disagreements arose between La Salle and the leading men of the colony. A captain of one of the vessels set sail for France, carrying away most of the ammunition. Finally, the settlement was abandoned, and a new location was selected on the Lavaca

River, and a fort was there erected, and named St. Louis, in honor of the king.

La Salle, the leading spirit of this infant colony, being of an adventurous disposition, and being intensely desirous of ascertaining the exact mouth of the great Mississippi River, started on the business of exploring the vast regions between Texas and Illinois; and after enduring incredible hardships, and meeting with many wild and romantic adventures, was finally murdered by one of his own men. The Indians, on hearing of La Salle's death, attacked Fort St. Louis, and killed or scattered all the colonists. This was the end of the first European colony in Texas.

THE FIRST WHITE MAN LOST IN TEXAS.

In 1720, a colony of Europeans entered the Gulf of Mexico, with the view of settling in Louisiana. Among them was M. de Belisle, a gentleman of distinction. The wind and current carried the vessel on which he was sailing into Matagorda Bay. A boat was sent ashore for water, and Belisle, with four others, went in it. As the boat had to make several trips to and from the ship during the day, these men concluded to remain on shore and go out hunting. But, overstaying their time, the boat made the last trip, and the captain, becoming impatient, weighed anchor and sailed from the Bay. Being thus left alone in an unknown country, the hunters traveled westward along the coast for several days, living upon herbs and insects. Belisle had brought a young dog with him from the vessel. This he gave up to one of the men to be killed for food. The man was so weak with hunger that he was unable to kill him, and the dog escaped and disappeared. The four companions of Belisle died of starvation and despair before his eyes; and for some days after, he continued to live on worms and insects, until at last the dog returned with an opossum which he had killed. Shortly after this, the dog was wounded by a wild beast, and he was compelled to kill him. Being thus left alone, he turned from the west, and bent his course to the interior, in search of men. He found footsteps, and followed them to a river, on the opposite side of which he saw some Indians engaged in drying meat. They soon discovered him, caught him, stripped him, and divided his clothes among them. They then took him to their village, and gave him to an old squaw, who treated him so kindly, that he soon recovered his strength. He learned their language, became a warrior, and rose to distinction among them.

After some time, a party of strange Indians visited the tribe where he was a captive, and, seeing him, remarked that they had also in their nation some men of the same color. This remark excited Belisle's feelings, and he determined to profit by it. He then made some ink of soot, and wrote on a piece of paper which he had secretly saved, an account of his condition. One of the strange Indians secretly agreed to carry it to the white people at Natchitoches. He performed his promise, delivered the paper to Captain St. Denis, commandant of that post, who wept on learning the fate of his white brother. As St. Denis was a great friend of the Indians, and a favorite with them, ten of their number volunteered to go after Belisle, and return in two moons. They were furnished with horses, and a horse, arms, and clothing for the prisoner. They reached the village, and fired off their guns, which overawed the Indians. Then delivering a letter from St. Denis to Belisle, they helped him to mount his horse, and the whole party galloped away, and reached Natchitoches in safety. From there Belisle found his way to the infant city of New Orleans, and became Major General of the Marine of Louisiana.

THE SPANIARDS IN TEXAS.

Early in 1686, the Spaniards, who at this time held possession of Mexico, hearing of the effort of the French, under La Salle, to make settlements in Texas, determined on driving them out of the country. An expedition of one hundred men left the Spanish settlement of Monclava in the spring of 1689. But on arriving at Fort St. Louis, on the Lavaca, they found it abandoned. Going into the country, they found two of the French colonists among the Cenis Indians, whom they took prisoners, and sent to Mexico, and there condemned to work in the mines. Returning to Fort St. Louis, they there established the Mission of San Francisco; and collecting some priests and friars, commenced their efforts to convert the Indians. The king of Spain now determined to recover the possession of all Texas and Coahuila. A governor of the country was accordingly appointed; soldiers and priests were sent out to different points, to establish military posts and missions. They took with them cattle, and seeds for planting. They formed settlements on the Red River, the Neches, and the Guadalupe. But in a short time, all these infant colonies, and also that of Fort St. Louis, began to decline. The Indians were hostile, the crops failed, and the cattle died. So that in 1693, they were all abandoned, and Texas was once more without any European settlers.

Not much was done by the Spaniards after this to settle Texas, until the year 1715. From this year may be dated its permanent occupation by Spain. They now commenced in good earnest to found colonies, to establish missions. and by arms, agriculture and arts, to extend and establish their influence and laws over the whole country. But notwithstanding all their efforts and sacrifices, the Government was not prosperous; and in the year 1745, the entire Spanish population in Texas did not exceed fifteen hundred, with perhaps an equal number of converted Indians. In 1758, a sad scene occurred at San Saba. The Indians, in large numbers, assaulted the mission, and murdered priests, soldiers, and Indian converts, leaving not one alive to tell the tale. This fearful butchery caused the Spanish missions in Texas everywhere to decline. They never recovered from the blow.

During the American Revolution, the Spanish possessions of Mexico and Texas remained in quiet. Texas was safe from danger. Her harbors were almost unknown; her property offered no temptation to pillage, and her scattered population could afford no recruits. The Spanish settlement at Natchez, however, had opened up a trade with Texas through Nacogdoches. This road had become familiar to many besides the Spaniards. Traders, on their return, would make known to the Americans in and around Natchez, the advantages of trade in Texas, the surpassing beauty and richness of the country, the abundance of the game, and a thousand other attractions to adventurers. Thus the tide of travel and of trade began to set in the direction of this new country about the beginning of the present century. The town of Nacogdoches soon became a place of much importance. Many persons of wealth and education emigrated from Louisiana to that place. The old missionary station became a town. An arsenal, barracks, and other substantial buildings soon made their appearance—some of which are still standing.

Although the Spaniards held the country for upwards of one hundred and fifty years, yet little now exists in

Texas to remind us of their rule here, excepting the names which they gave to the principal towns and rivers. Most of these names are still retained.

AMERICANS IN TEXAS.

A trader, called Philip Nolan, engaged in traffic between Natchez (Mississippi) and San Antonio, about the year 1785. In October, 1800, he started on one of his expeditions into Texas, with a company of about twenty men. Among them was Ellis P. Bean, a young man of seventeen years of age, whose romantic character and strange adventures entitle him to a more extended notice. Nolan and his company, in order to avoid attracting public attention, took a new route, after crossing the Mississippi at Natchez. Occasionally they halted to kill game and refresh themselves. Before reaching Red River, three of them strayed off, got lost, but afterwards found their way back to Natchez. Nolan and his remaining men passed around the head of Lake Bistineau, and crossing Red River, came to a Caddo village, where they obtained some fine horses. In ten days they crossed the Trinity, and immediately entered upon an immense rolling prairie, through which they advanced, till they came to a spring, which they named the *Painted Spring*. At the head of this spring stood a rock, painted by the Indians, to commemorate a treaty which had once been made there.

In the vast prairie around them they could find no fuel with which to cook their food. The buffalo, once so numerous here, had all disappeared, and they were compelled to live for nine days on the flesh of *mustang* horses. By this time they reached the Brazos, where they found plenty of deer, elk, and "wild horses by thousands." Here they built an enclosure, and caught and penned three hundred head of mustangs. At this place, they were visited by two hundred Camanche Indians, with whom they went on a visit to the great chief Necoroco, on the south bank of Red River, where they remained a month, making many friends, and gaining much information. They returned at length to their old camp, accompanied by an escort of the natives, who managed to steal eleven of their best American horses.

The company at this time consisted of Captain Nolan, five Spaniards, eleven Americans, and one negro. As they could do nothing without their horses, some six of the company volunteered to go after them. They went on foot, and after a march of nine days found four of the horses, under the care of a few Indians. The other horses, the Indians said, had been taken on a buffalo-hunt by the balance of their party, and would return in the evening. They further stated that the one who stole the horses was a one-eyed Indian chief. In the evening, the Indians came in, bringing the horses and abundance of meat. The whites tied the one-eyed chief, and guarded him till morning; they then took such provisions as they wanted for their journey, let the Indians go, and returned to their camp in four days.

While in camp, resting themselves, a troop of one hundred and fifty Spaniards came suddenly upon them. The trampling of the horses aroused the Americans, who, seeing their danger, prepared for defense. They had built a square inclosure of logs, in which they slept at night. Into this they fled. The Spaniards at daybreak commenced their fire, which was returned from the log pen. In ten minutes, Captain Nolan was killed by a ball in the head. Bean then took the command, and continued the fight. In a short time after, two more of the little company fell. The Spaniards had brought with them a swivel on the back of a mule, with which they fired grape. At this time, Bean proposed to his men to charge on this piece of artillery, but the men jointly opposed it. It was next proposed to retreat, which was agreed to. Each one filled his powder-horn, and the remaining ammunition was placed in charge of the negro. They left the inclosure, and gained a small creek. While here engaged in fighting, the negro with the ammunition, and one wounded man, stopped and surrendered. Bean and his party, though under a constant fire from the enemy on both sides, kept up the fight, until at last they took refuge in a ravine, and, for a short time, the firing ceased. At length the enemy began to close in upon the ravine, but were soon repulsed. About two o'clock in the afternoon, the Spaniards hoisted a white flag, and an American, who was with the Spaniards, was appointed to hold a parley with Bean. They said, all they desired was, that the Americans would return to their homes, and cease to come any more into Texas. The Americans agreed to this. A treaty was made, in which it was agreed that both parties should return together to Nacogdoches—the Americans not to surrender, but to retain their arms.

They soon reached the Trinity River, which was overflowing its banks. Bean soon contrived to make a small canoe out of a dry cotton-wood tree, and managed to carry over all the Spaniards, leaving their arms and commander on the other side. He now proposed to his men to throw the arms into the river, start the commander over, and again march for the prairies. In this, however, he was not seconded.

In a few days they all reached Nacogdoches, where they remained a month, expecting, according to promise, to be sent home. But in violation of the treaty, they were all put in irons and sent to San Antonio. Here they were kept in prison three months. They were then sent to San Louis Potosi, where they remained in prison for sixteen months. The prisoners being without clothes, contrived means to procure them. Bean and Charles King gave themselves out as shoemakers, and were permitted to work at their prison doors, by which means they earned some money. Then they were started off to Chihuahua. Arriving at Saltillo, they were treated with more kindness. Their irons were taken off, and they were permitted to walk about the town. Here we will leave them for the present, simply remarking, that this battle of twelve Americans with one hundred and fifty mounted Spaniards, was probably the first which ever took place between these two nations, and from it we may judge of the character of each.

FIRST AMERICAN COLONY IN TEXAS.

The first grant from the Mexican Government to found an American colony in Texas, was dated January 17, 1821. This grant was given to Moses Austin, a native of Connecticut, and the father of the distinguished Colonel Stephen F. Austin. The father dying suddenly, the son undertook the great and benevolent work of carrying out his father's plans. He accordingly explored the country watered by the Guadalupe, Colorado, and Brazos Rivers, and laid out the town of San Felipe de Austin, on the Brazos. The news of Austin's colony had spread over the western country, and there were many adventurers who were anxious to join him; so that the number of colonists came on faster than provision could be made for their support. The first settlers were often reduced to the necessity of living entirely on wild game, and clothing themselves with skins. They also suffered greatly for several years from the Carankaw Indians. In the year 1813, one of the colonists gives us the following account of their sufferings:

"Those of us who have no families live with families

of the settlement. A part of us are obliged to go out in the morning to hunt food, leaving a part of the men behind to protect the women and children from the Indians. Game is now so scarce that we often hunt a whole day for a deer or turkey, and return at night empty-handed. It would make your heart sick to see the poor little half-naked children, who have eaten nothing during the day, watch for the return of the hunters at night. As soon as they catch the first glimpse of them, they eagerly run out to meet them, and learn if they have found any game. If the hunters return with a deer or turkey, the children are wild with delight. But if they return without food, the little creatures suddenly stop in their course, and the big tears start and roll down their pale cheeks."

These were hard times for the young colony. But they were engaged in a great and good work, and met and overcame all difficulties with manly firmness. The common dress of the people was buckskin; and occasionally a strolling peddler would penetrate into the wilderness with a piece of domestic or calico, which was deemed of as much elegance as silk or satin is among us.

Soon after the establishment of Austin's colony, many other colonies were founded in different parts of the country. The settlement at Victoria was begun in 1825. The town of Gonzales was laid off about the same time. In 1828, Colonel Austin obtained another contract to colonize three hundred families on lands near the Gulf. Texas had now become the great point of attraction to thousands of adventurers from all parts of the United States. Men of desperate fortunes and of roving habits, speculators in land, broken-down politicians, refugees from justice, as well as multitudes of a better class, who were desirous of finding new homes for their growing families, and fresh lands for their increasing slaves, swelled the tide of Texas immigration. This tide, rolling down from the Northern and Western states, at last excited the jealousy of the Mexican government, and finally brought on a war with Mexico, which ended in the independence of Texas.

GALVESTON ISLAND.

From the discovery of this island, in 1686, by the French under La Salle, until 1816, it remained unsettled. A few roving Indians occasionally resorted to the western end of the island for the purpose of fishing, but there were no human habitations on it. As late as 1816, it was covered with a long, green grass, on which fed herds of deer. It also abounded in serpents, and was hence called by the pirates of the Gulf, *Snake Island.* In 1816, Don Louis Aury, commodore of the fleet of the Republics of Mexico, Venezuela, La Plata, and New Granada, consisting of fifteen small vessels, was chosen governor of the province of Texas and Galveston Island. He immediately set out upon a cruise against Spanish commerce, and soon swept from the Gulf the vessels of the mother country. The rich prizes brought into Galveston soon enabled Aury and his little garrison to live handsomely. African slaves were also smuggled into the place, and sold at about one hundred and fifty dollars apiece, and sent across the country into Louisiana. In 1817, it fell into the possession of the celebrated Lafitte, who had for many years been the terror of the Gulf—a man of great accomplishments and of many crimes—who, when the war between England and the United States broke out in 1812, had his headquarters at Barataria, in Louisiana, and after refusing to join the British, offered his services to the American Government, was pardoned by the Legislature of Louisiana, and fought bravely at the battle of New Orleans under General Jackson.

After the battle of New Orleans, Lafitte returned to his former occupation, and he and his followers on Galveston Island numbered nearly a thousand men. They were of all nations and languages, and though pretending to be engaged, under their distinguished leader, as privateers, were actually nothing but pirates. Lafitte was a man of handsome person, winning manners, generous disposition, and had a wonderful influence over his men. He built his town on the ruins of Aury's village, erected a dwelling called the *red house*, and constructed a fort, a small arsenal and dock-yard. From New Orleans he was supplied with building materials, provisions, and many of the luxuries of life. A "Yankee" boarding-house sprung up, and Galveston soon became a place of many attractions to the wild free-booters of the Gulf. But, in 1820, Lafitte and his men committed some acts which brought on him the displeasure of the United States Government, who sent an armed vessel and broke up his establishment. This prince of pirates entertained the captain of the American vessel with great hospitality at the *red house*. He then assembled his followers, made them an address, supplied them with money, advised them to disperse, and bidding the American officer farewell, sailed out of the bay, and left Galveston forever.

Galveston, in 1822, was again desolate, and for some years it was only visited occasionally by sailors in search of Lafitte's hidden treasures. In 1836, the eastern end of the Island was occupied by some Texas troops under Colonel Morgan, who had charge of some Mexican prisoners. Two years after this, when Texas had established its independence, and crowds of strangers commenced coming into the country, the town began to rise in importance. Commerce had sought out the harbor as the best in the young Republic, and responsible merchants began to make it their permanent abode. In 1838, vessels were arriving and departing daily, and the harbor presented the appearance of an Atlantic port. In the first quarter of the year 1840, ninety-two vessels arrived at the port of Galveston.

THE FALL OF THE ALAMO.

In 1836, Santa Anna, who was at that time President of Mexico, determined to invade Texas, and either drive the Americans out of the country, or crush out the spirit of independence which had broken out among them. Accordingly he set out for the Rio Grande on the 1st of February of that year, at the head of seven thousand troops, and on the 27th of the same month, he marched into the city of San Antonio. The few Texas soldiers who were stationed in that city retired across the river in good order, and took refuge in the Alamo. The Alamo, though strong, was not properly a fort, but a presidio or mission. It had been standing for nearly one hundred and fifty years, and had been the scene of many strange and interesting events. Here Colonel Travis, with his small force of not more than one hundred and fifty men, determined to make a stand, and conquer or die. He had only eight cannon, and was greatly deficient in provisions and ammunition. When the enemy first appeared before the place, he had only ninety bushels of corn and thirty head of cattle. But the watch-word of the little band of heroes was, "Victory or death!" Santa Anna immediately demanded a surrender, which was answered by a shot from the fort. The enemy then hoisted the red flag, and commenced the attack. They erected a number of batteries, and for several days kept up a constant skirmishing. Travis and his little band frequently sallied out and met their assailants, whom they drove back with considerable loss. On the 1st of March, thirty-two gallant men, from Gonzales, forced their way into the Alamo, thus swelling the force of Travis to one hundred and eighty-eight. For several succeeding days the contest was kept up with spirit on both sides, the Texans firing but seldom, in order to save their ammunition; and the Mexicans advancing their batteries nearer and nearer to the walls. Travis succeeded in sending out, through the enemy's lines, a last appeal to his country for help in this his terrible extremity, setting forth his position, and stating that if not soon reinforced, he and his men had solemnly determined to perish in the struggle. By the same courier he wrote to a friend in Washington County the following affecting message: "Take care of my little boy. If the country is saved, I may make him a fortune. But if all is lost, and I shall perish, I will leave him nothing but the proud recollection that he is the son of a man who died for his country."

Thus for one long week did this little band of heroes defend themselves against the overwhelming force of the enemy, until they were completely worn down by constant watching and fighting. On Sunday morning, the 6th of March, Santa Anna determined to take the place by storm, and the Alamo was completely surrounded by the whole Mexican army. The infantry was placed in a circle nearest the fort, and the cavalry around them, so that not a single straggler might escape. At a given signal, the whole host advanced rapidly, under a tremendous fire from the Texans. Just at daylight, ladders were placed against the walls, and the soldiers began to climb up. But they were hurled down by the brave defenders within. Again the charge was sounded, and a second effort made to reach the top of the wall; but again the assailants were beaten back. For a few minutes there was a pause. A third attempt was made with more success. Some reached the top of the wall, wavered and fell; but their places were supplied by hundreds pressing up behind them on every ladder. At last, cut down, killed and wounded, the Texan defenders began to give way. Instantly the fort was filled with hundreds of infuriated murderers. The survivors within the walls still continued the battle. They clubbed their guns, and with shouts and yells of defiance, fought from wall to wall, from room to room. Some few cried for quarter, but no quarter was given. Travis and Crockett fell with piles of dead Mexicans around them. Major Evans, in attempting to set fire to the magazine, was shot down. Colonel Bowie, who was sick in his bed, was murdered and his body mangled. Major Dickinson, in attempting to leap from the wall with his child tied on his back, was instantly killed. Thus, one by one those noble heroes sold their lives; and by sunrise on that Sabbath morn, every one had perished, and all was still. But around them lay the dead bodies of over five hundred Mexicans, with an equal number of wounded.

The only survivors of this terrible conflict were Mrs. Dickinson, her child, a negro servant of Colonel Travis, and two Mexican women. The bodies of the Texans were stripped, mutilated, and then thrown into heaps and burnt.

As not one of all the defenders of the Alamo escaped, we shall never know the full particulars of that desperate struggle.

About a year after, their bones and ashes were collected, placed in a coffin, and buried with due solemnity. A small monument was made from the stones of the fortress in 1841, was purchased by the State, and now stands in the Capitol at Austin. But the most lasting monument of the heroes of the Alamo is found in the hearts of their countrymen, who will cherish their memory, and tell each succeeding generation the tale of their sufferings, their endurance, and their heroic end.

> They fell unnoticed, but undying—
> The very gales their names seem sighing.

CAPTURE AND SLAUGHTER OF FANNIN'S MEN AT GOLIAD.

The news of the fall of the Alamo and the entire destruction of its brave defenders soon spread throughout Texas. It now became necessary that the army of the young republic should retreat before the advance of the larger force under Santa Anna, and make a stand against him in the eastern part of the country. Accordingly, General Houston, who was at the time at Gonzales, issued orders that the scattered troops should fall back and unite at some more favorable place. In this retreat the two armies had frequent skirmishes, in some of which the Texans gained signal advantages.

Colonel Fannin, who was stationed at Goliad with three hundred men, began his retreat. Thinking that the enemy would not pursue him, he was not sufficiently on his guard, and was overtaken at the Coleta Creek, about thirty miles east of Goliad, on the 20th of March. He and his men were in an open prairie, and the infantry and cavalry of the enemy were concealed in the timber near the creek. The enemy's cavalry, coming up within a quarter of a mile, dismounted, and began to advance and fire. Fannin ordered his men to reserve their fire and to lie down in the grass. The Mexicans having now come within one hundred yards, the Texans opened a fire of rifles, muskets, and artillery. Fannin here received a flesh wound in the leg.

While thus engaged with the Mexican cavalry on their right flank, they suddenly discovered the enemy's infantry, one thousand strong, advancing on their left and rear, and concealing themselves in the long grass. Whenever they would rise to shoot, and show their heads, the Texas rifles generally took them down. The battle soon became general. The Texans having no water to sponge their cannon, the pieces soon became so hot that they could not use them, and they were forced to rely wholly on their small arms. With these they kept up the fight from one o'clock until sundown. At dusk, a party of Camanche Indians, who had joined the Mexicans, were placed in the high grass, about thirty yards from the Texans, from which they poured a destructive fire. But, as soon as it became sufficiently dark for the Texans to see the flash of their guns, they seldom flashed twice from the same place. A little after dark, the enemy drew off their troops.

The Texans lost, during the day, seven killed and sixty wounded. The enemy's loss must have been five times as great.

The Mexicans took position, during the night, in the skirt of the woods. Early in the morning they renewed the attack, and, arranging their whole force in the most imposing manner, surrounded the little band of Texans with overwhelming numbers. Fannin and his officers now held a consultation, and it was the opinion of the majority that they should surrender. A white flag was raised, and terms were agreed on. It was stipulated that the Texans should be received as prisoners of war, and in eight days should be sent to the coast and shipped to the United States. This agreement was reduced to writing in both the English and Spanish languages, read over two or three times, and the writing exchanged "in the most formal and solemn manner."

The Texans immediately stacked their arms and such of them as were able to walk, were marched back to Goliad on the same day. At Goliad they were crowded into the old church, with no other food than a little beef, without bread or salt. Some other prisoners were also brought in who had been captured at other points. Here they were kept until the 27th of the month, expecting every day to leave for the United States. The prisoners were spending the evening of the 27th in the most pleasant manner. Colonel Fannin was entertaining his friends with the prospect of a speedy return to the United States; and some of the young men, who could perform well on the flute, were singing "Home, Sweet Home." Alas! how little they knew of the sad fate that was awaiting them. At seven o'clock at night, a courier arrived with an order from Santa Anna, that the prisoners should all be shot! Accordingly, on the next morning at the dawn of day, the Texans were awakened by a Mexican officer, who said he wished them to form a line that they might be counted. The men were marched out in several divisions, under different pretexts. Some were told that they were to be taken to Copano, to be sent immediately home; others, that they were going out to kill beeves; and others again, that they were being removed from the church to make room for Santa Anna and his suite. Dr. Shackleford, who had been reserved as a surgeon for the wounded Mexicans, and was invited to the tent of a Mexican officer, a little distance from the fort, says: "In about half an hour we heard the report of a volley of small arms on the east of the fort. I immediately inquired the cause of the firing. The officer replied that he did not know, but supposed it was the guard firing off their guns. In about fifteen or twenty minutes after, another such volley was heard directly south of us. At the same time I could distinguish the heads of some of the men through the branches of some peach-trees, and could hear their screams. It was then, for the first time, that the awful conviction seized upon our minds, that *treachery* and *murder* had begun their work. I then asked the officer if it could be possible they were murdering our men. He replied that it was so, but that *he* had not given the order, neither had executed it. In about an hour more the wounded were dragged out and butchered. Colonel Fannin was the last to suffer. When informed of his fate, he met it like a soldier. He handed his watch to the man who was to kill him, and requested him to shoot him in the head, and not in the back. He then seated himself in a chair, tied a handkerchief over his eyes, bared his bosom, and received the fire.

"As different divisions were brought to the place of execution, they were ordered to sit down with their backs to the guard. A young man, of the name of Fenner, rose on his feet, and exclaimed, 'Boys, they are going to kill us—die with your faces to them, like men!' At the same time, two other young men, swinging their caps over their heads, shouted at the top of their voices, 'Hurrah for Texas!'

"Many attempted to escape; but most of those who survived the first fire were pursued by the cavalry and cut down. It is believed that twenty-seven of those who were marched out to be slaughtered made their escape, leaving three hundred and thirty who were butchered in cold blood. The dead were then stripped, and their naked bodies thrown into piles, and though an attempt was made to burn them, it did not fully succeed, and many of them were left a prey to dogs and vultures."

Peace to the ashes of these noble martyrs of liberty!

They did not fall in vain. A cry for vengeance arose to Heaven. It rung through the land, and a terrible retribution overtook the cruel murderer and his army at the battle of San Jacinto.

BATTLE OF SAN JACINTO.

The battle of San Jacinto was the last and most important one which took place in the war between Texas and Mexico. Though the numbers engaged in it were not very large, yet the victory of the Texans was so great, that it brought the war to a close, and soon led to the independence of Texas. It was fought on Buffalo Bayou, and near San Jacinto River, in Harris county, on April 21, 1836. General Santa Anna, the President of Mexico, commanded the Mexicans, and General Houston led the Texans. The Mexicans numbered fifteen hundred men, and the Texans only about seven hundred. We need not describe the proud advance of the Mexican army, the retreat of the Texans, the burning of Harrisburg, the skirmishing on the 20th, and other incidents which took place before the battle.

General Houston called a council of war, and it was decided that they must now fight, or the Mexicans would drive them out of the country, and compel them to cross over into Louisiana. Many of the soldiers were impatient to bring the matter to close quarters, and were determined either to meet the enemy at once, or else go home and take care of their families and property, which were in danger of being destroyed by parties from the Mexican army, who were prowling over the country. It was about three o'clock on the afternoon of the 21st, when General Houston made preparations for the attack. The Mexicans seemed to be almost entirely unprepared for battle. They had just finished their dinner. Some were lounging about the camp. Some were playing monte, and many were taking a quiet nap. Santa Anna was himself asleep. The Texans formed their plan of attack behind the shelter of some trees, which concealed them from view. Burleson's regiment was placed in the center; Sherman's on the left wing, and the cavalry, under Lamar, on the extreme right. The artillery, including the "Twin Sisters," was under the charge of Hockley. The whole army was soon in readiness. The "Twin Sisters" now advanced to within two hundred yards of the Mexican breastworks, and opened a destructive fire with grape and canister. Sherman's regiment rushed forward and began the attack with great fury. The whole line then advanced in double-quick time, shouting, "Remember the Alamo!" "Remember Goliad!" The Mexicans fired as the Texans approached, but the latter reserved their fire until they were within pistol shot. They then opened fire along their whole line. The effect of this discharge was terrible. They made no halt. Onward they rushed, firing and yelling as they went. The Texan cavalry then charged that of the Mexicans, who immediately fled; and in a few minutes Burleson's regiment and Millard's infantry stormed the breastwork, and captured their whole artillery. In fifteen minutes after the charge, the Mexicans gave way at all points, and the pursuit became general. Some fled to the river; some to the swamp, and most of them to a clump of trees in their rear, where they surrendered. Such was their terror, and so sudden was their flight, that many of their cannon were left loaded, their money and other valuables left untouched.—Those that were asleep, awoke only to be overwhelmed or killed. Those that were cooking left their food untouched; and those that were playing monte, left the game unfinished. The swamp, in the rear of their camp, presented an awful scene. Men and horses, the dead and dying, were piled in heaps, and formed a bridge over which their terrible pursuers continued the chase. The Texans, not having time to load their guns, used them as clubs; and then, seizing their bowie-knives, slaughtered the poor fugitives like sheep. Many begged for their lives, but no quarter was given them. Their pursuers remembered the many fearful outrages committed by the Mexicans on former occasions, and they were determined to put to death all who came within their power.

At dark the pursuit of the flying enemy ceased. The prisoners who surrendered before the flight commenced, were conducted to the Texan camp, a guard placed over them, and were furnished with provisions. The wounded of both armies were cared for. In summing up the results of the battle, it was found that 630 Mexicans were killed, 208 wounded, and 103 made prisoners. A large quantity of arms, great numbers of mules and horses, camp equipage, and the army chest, containing $12,000, were captured. The Texans had only 8 killed and 25 wounded. General Houston received a wound in the leg.

On the morning of the 22d, detachments were sent out to scour the country in the direction towards Harrisburg, and pick up stragglers. A party of five continued their search down Buffalo Bayou. One of them, in the act of shooting a deer, saw a Mexican hiding in the tall grass, with a blanket over his head. They called to him to rise and come to them. He advanced, and taking one of them by the hand, kissed it. They asked him who he was. He replied that he was only a private soldier. But, seeing some gold buttons on his shirt, they pointed to them. He then burst into tears, and begged to be conducted to General Houston.

This prisoner was none other than the celebrated Santa Anna. On approaching Houston, he announced his name, and declared himself a prisoner of war. General Houston was reclining beneath a tree, and was suffering considerable pain from his wound. He, however, received the prisoner with due consideration. Santa Anna was much agitated and much alarmed. Knowing the hatred entertained towards him by the Texans, because of his many former cruelties, he justly feared their vengeance. He asked for opium, some of which he swallowed, whether for the purpose of quieting his nerves, or destroying his life, we know not. But in a few minutes he recovered his usual composure, and began to display his usual vanity. He at once made application to be released from captivity. "You," said he to Houston, "can afford to be generous, for you have conquered the Napoleon of the West!" General Houston distinctly informed him that he should be turned over to the civil authorities. President Burnett then took charge of him; and after detaining him for some time a prisoner, he was permitted to go to Washington City, from whence he was sent home by General Jackson, in a vessel of war, to Vera Cruz.

Thus ended the celebrated battle of San Jacinto. The brave band, under their distinguished leader, obtained a victory as glorious as any other recorded in the annals of history, and the happy consequences of it will be felt in Texas in all future generations. It shows what brave men can do when fighting for liberty against tyrants.

RELIGION IN TEXAS.

Although many of the early settlers in Texas were immoral in their habits, yet the mass of the people entertained a great regard for religious observances.

Most of them were educated in the older States, and brought with them their reverence for sacred things. The leading men among them were well aware that no people can be prosperous who do not encourage the worship of God. This was particularly true after the country became independent of Mexico. It was then that a feeling of gratitude to Heaven, for its blessing on their efforts to become a free people, seemed to pervade all classes, and ministers of the Gospel, of all denominations, were cordially welcomed to the country. It is now difficult to decide what Christian sect had the honor of organizing the first church in Texas. The Methodists and Baptists both claim this distinction.

As early as 1818, the Rev. Henry Stephenson, of the Methodist denomination, preached in the Red River settlements, in Western Louisiana. In 1824 he paid a visit to Texas, and preached the first Protestant sermon west of the Brazos, near San Felipe. There were four families present on that occasion. The first campmeeting was held in Texas in 1833, ten miles from San Augustine. About eighty persons attended. A few individuals professed religion, and a church was organized. On January 17, 1838, the corner-stone of a Methodist house of worship was laid in San Augustine. Gen. Thomas J. Rusk delivered an address on the occasion. This was the first effort to erect a church building west of the Sabine.

In 1837, the Rev. R. Alexander, D.D., emigrated to Texas, preached extensively throughout the State, was the means of doing a great amount of good, and still lives to see the fruits of his labors. About the same time, the Rev. Dr. Ruter, for some time president of Alleghany College in Pennsylvania, a man of practical views, sound learning, and of a truly missionary spirit, settled within the bounds of the young republic, and labored and died in Texas.

One of the most remarkable preachers, whose name appears in the early history of the State, was Paul Denton. He was early left an orphan in Arkansas, and lived in a family where he was treated as a servant, and had to cook, wash, scour, and perform other degrading work. Until he was twelve years of age, he was a stranger to hat and shoes. When he became older, he ran away from his oppressors, and commenced life for himself. At an early age he married, and learned to read and write after becoming the head of a family. He finally became a preacher, and soon showed remarkable powers as a public speaker. He was a man of fine person, agreeable manners, and although without any advantages of education, displayed a high degree of eloquence. His first efforts as a preacher of the Gospel were in the Red Lands in Eastern Texas. He afterwards removed to the northern part of the State. He was a man of public spirit, and was brave as well as good. He raised a company of volunteers to chastise the Indians, who had become troublesome to the white settlers, and was killed in battle. Texas has honored him in calling a county by his name.

Among other ministers of the Gospel who came to Texas at an early time the Rev. Sumner Bacon is worthy of honorable notice. He arrived in the country in 1828. He was a native of Massachusetts, and was first a soldier in the United States army before he became a clergyman. He was a man of great energy and courage. In connection with his duties as a preacher, he distributed thousands of copies of the Bible from the Sabine to San Antonio. On one occasion he was overtaken by a band of ruffians, who seized him and threatened him with instant death. He begged his captors to first join with him in prayer. They refused to unite with him, but consented that he might first pray himself before they put their threat into execution. He knelt down and prayed so fervently, that they all quietly left him. On another occasion, as he and some others were preparing to hold religious services near San Antonio, certain persons sent him word that they intended to come and break up the meeting. Col. James Bowie, being in the neighborhood, and hearing of their purpose, went to the place where the meeting was to be held. He made the sign of the cross on the ground, and informed them that he was captain in those parts, and that the meeting should take place. Knowing the character of Bowie, and fearing his wrath, the opposers of the meeting withdrew, and Bacon and his friends proceeded with their services. Mr. Bacon belonged to the Cumberland Presbyterian Church.

ANIMALS OF TEXAS.

A stranger, on first arriving in Texas, is struck with the large size and spreading horns of the cattle. Their large and superior forms are probably owing to the mild climate and the abundance of grass, which yields a rich supply of food at all seasons of the year. They require no other care than occasional herding to keep them gentle and prevent their straying, and to mark the calves.

Hogs thrive admirably in Texas on grass, roots, mast, and fruits. Pork is easily converted into bacon, and preserved without difficulty, owing greatly to the peculiar dryness of the air.

Herds of wild horses feed on the prairies, and increase in numbers as you proceed west. They are easily subdued to the saddle. The catching of a wild horse by a Mexican is a display of skill and valor which is truly wonderful. The ranchero on horseback dashes among the herd as they rush over the prairie, and swinging about his head his *lariat*—a platted rawhide with a running noose at the end—he throws it with great accuracy over the neck of the wild animal, and in a few minutes he is run down and captured. Mules are also raised in great numbers, though perhaps not so good as those of Kentucky.

No country surpasses Texas in abundance of game. Immense herds of buffalo were still found, within a few years past, in the northwestern settlements. Deer flock over every prairie. Wild turkeys, the prairie hen, partridges, the delicate rice-bird, with numerous others, are found in great numbers. During the winter, the bays are alive with thousands of wild geese and ducks. The flamingo is occasionally seen to display its brilliant plumage. The stately swan frequents the waters of the bays; and around the houses of the plantations the mocking-bird sings its melodious notes.

In all the waters, fish, of the choicest kind, abound. Along the coast are oysters of the largest size and finest flavor.

The fiercest wild animal in Texas is probably the panther, though it is rarely met with. There are also bears, wolves and a few wild-cats. Among the lesser animals are the opossum, rabbit, and gray squirrel.

EARLY CHURCHES IN TEXAS.

In a previous article it will be seen that the Methodist Church sent the largest number of clergymen, in early times, to Texas.

The first Baptist preacher who came to the country, was the Rev. Joseph Bays, who emigrated from Missouri, and preached on Peach Creek, on the west side of the Brazos, in the year 1826. In a short time he removed to San Antonio, where he continued to labor until he was ordered away by the Mexican authorities. In 1829, a number of Baptists, who came from New York, established the first Sabbath-school in the country, in the town of San Felipe. It was taught by T. J. Pilgrim, who was the interpreter of the Spanish language in Austin's colony. The same year another Sabbath-school was opened at Matagorda, and in the year following a similar one was started at "Old Caney," by members of the same Church. After this time, many members and ministers of the Baptist Church came to the country and organized churches in different parts of the State.

In the year 1838, the Rev. Caleb S. Ives, of the Protestant Episcopal Church, arrived at Matagorda, where he collected a congregation, established a school, and built a church. He continued to labor until 1849, when he died. In the fall of 1838, the Rev. R. M. Chapman, of the same Church, came to Houston and organized a parish. In 1840, he was succeeded by Rev. H. B. Godwin.

In the spring of 1840, the Rt. Rev. Leonidas Polk (late General Polk of the Confederate army) visited and explored the country between the Trinity and the Colorado. In 1844, the Rt. Rev. G. W. Freeman, Bishop of Arkansas, visited the churches of Texas, and continued his visits annually for several years. In 1841, the Rev. B. Eaton was sent out, as a missionary, to Galveston and Houston. On January 1, 1849, a separate diocese was organized for Texas with six clergymen. Since that time the Episcopal Church has continued to grow both in numbers and influence.

The Presbyterian Church was not among the pioneer churches in Texas. About the year 1838, the Rev.

Hugh Wilson arrived in the new republic. He was probably the first Presbyterian minister who settled in Texas. He organized a Presbyterian Church in San Augustine shortly after his arrival, and in the year following established one at Independence. He was a laborious and useful man, and will always stand high among the first ministers of the Gospel in Texas. The Rev. John McCulloch came to Galveston about the same time, and gathered a congregation and founded a Sabbath-school under many disadvantages. The state of morals and religion in the Island City at that time was not very favorable to the efforts of the young missionary.*

With the Rev. W. Y. Allen, at Houston, and Rev. W. C. Blair, P. H. Fullenwider, I. J. Henderson, F. Rutherford, and a few others, located at different points in the State, the Presbyterian Church began, about the year 1840, to take a position among the other religious denominations in the country, and has been gradually advancing in influence and usefulness until the present time. As most of the clergymen referred to are still living, we can say but little more respecting them than merely to give their names.

The most laborious and useful minister of the Presbyterian Church, who ever lived in Texas, was the Rev. Dr. Baker, who died within a few years past at Austin. He was a man of great energy and apostolic zeal. All could see that his sole aim and purpose was to preach the Gospel and do good to the souls of men. Coming to Texas as a missionary about the year 1840, he visited almost every part of the State, and preached most abundantly. In all weathers and in all places, he showed himself the fearless soldier of the cross. With a fine

* Mr. McCulloch died within the last three years.

person, a silvery voice, and often with melting eyes, he presented the great truths of salvation in such a manner as to attract large congregations, and win many converts to Christ. At last, after a long and useful ministry, he died a peaceful and happy death in the city of Austin. The college at Huntsville owes its existence to his exertions.

LETTER FROM NASHVILLE.

THE TEXAS DEAD AT THE BATTLE OF FRANKLIN.

NASHVILLE, Tennessee, *Nov.* 26, 1867.

BEING in attendance as a delegate from Texas to the Southern General Assembly of the Presbyterian Church now in session in this city, I accepted an invitation a few days ago to visit the mansion of Colonel John McGavock at Franklin, twenty miles from Nashville, that I might partake of his princely hospitality and view the quiet resting-place of those Southern soldiers who fell in the disastrous battle of Franklin on the 30th of December, 1864. Three Louisiana friends accompanied me. Here repose, in peaceful graves, the mortal remains of nearly fifteen hundred Confederate soldiers who fell on that eventful day. Around their silent dust an elegant iron fence is now near its completion, erected by the citizens of Galveston, Houston, and the surrounding villages, through the agency of Miss Gay, of Georgia, whose presence in Houston some months ago will be remembered by many, and whose faithful disbursement of the funds contributed, together with the names of every Texian contributor, is attested by documents now in the hands of Colonel McGavock. In full view of the mansion, and on a gently-sloping lawn, we entered the gate, and paced solemnly down the smooth walk that separates the long rows of rounded hillocks where, in regular order, are interred the remains of Mississippians and Tennesseans, soldiers from Georgia, Alabama, and Texas—each in his warrior bed, on which is inscribed the name, company, and former residence of the occupant. With emotions which patriotic and Christian hearts alone can fully feel, and with silent tears on the cheeks of men not used to weep, we advanced from grave to grave. We thought of the bloody strife and of these sad results. Here lies the mangled body of many a father who came far from home to fight the battles of his country; of many a son, the pride of his mother; of many a brother, the idol of fond sisters, and many more, bound to distant ones by still tenderer and holier ties.

But the largest share of our attention and the deepest sympathy of our hearts were elicited, as we stopped and lingered long around that portion of the ground where lie the dead from Texas. There are fifty-nine in all, with the name of the Lone Star State inscribed on each tablet. Here they lie, far from home, and many a heart was left desolate by their fall. How grateful should those Texas parents feel, whose sons were spared through many a bloody conflict, and are now at their happy firesides, cheering their households by their presence, and cultivating the arts of peace. Why were these taken and others left? Why did my friend's son fall and mine escape? "Even so, Father, for so it seemed good in thy sight."

But we would not omit to say, that on many of the tablets of the Texas dead no name is lettered; but in its stead is simply the word "*Unknown!*"—unknown, alas, his name, his age, his calling—unknown the place where his kindred dwell—and unknown to kindred where lies the body of their lost Texan! As the sad word "unknown" was repeated with a low and saddened voice which I thought none near me could hear, the imposing form of an old friend (not of the clerical profession) advanced to my side, and with quivering lips uttered these cheering words:

> "'Unknown' is all the epitaph can tell—
> If Jesus knew thee—all is well."

I now looked around and inquired where lie the remains of General Granberry—that man of classic taste, and commanding form, and trumpet voice—Granberry, once my pupil, who sat in my recitation-room for four full years, in the quiet groves of Oakland College. "He is not yet here," replied our host; "but as soon as his Texas friends shall request his removal from a neighboring farm, he shall come here also, to repose among his friends who fell with him on the field of battle."

To those in Texas who have friends buried in this attractive spot, I would add that if they have inquiries to make, or requests to present respecting their dead, they may communicate without reserve with Colonel McGavock, the proprietor of the premises, who will cheerfully and promptly impart all needed information. And to some who may ask to be more fully informed respecting the agency of Miss Gay, who presented the claims of the cemetery to their consideration, I may add that no one more worthy of their confidence could have been selected to convey their offerings to the place designated.

THE

FIRST PROTESTANT EPISCOPAL SERMON

PREACHED IN NEW ORLEANS.

THE Rev. Benjamin Chase, D.D., of eighty years of age, the oldest Presbyterian clergyman of the South-west, recently deceased at Natchez, in a letter dated November 28, 1869, writes as follows:

"The Rev. Jedediah Smith was a Congregational minister, with twelve children, ten of whom accompanied him from Granville, Massachusetts, to the Natchez country, in 1776. On his way, landing at what was called the Island of Orleans, under the dominion of Spain, he was there seized by the Romish priesthood, all his property was confiscated, and his library burned on the levee.

"After his release he obtained a keel-boat, and with the aid of his sons slowly and tediously ascended the Mississippi, in the month of July, as far as Loftus Heights, now Fort Adams. Exposed to the midsummer sun, and unaccustomed to the climate, he was taken sick, and the boat was left to the management of his sons, who conducted it to Natchez, where he died soon after his arrival, and was buried below the Bluff, not far from Fort Rosalie. In a few years the bank of the river broke away, and ever afterwards rendered the place of his interment unknown. Six of his sons, viz., William, Josephus, Philetus, Israel, Philander, and Calvin, with two daughters, Sarah and Philomela, settled on Second and St. Catharine Creeks, within eight or ten miles from Natchez, became wealthy, influential and highly re-spectable families, and many of their children and descendants became members of the Presbyterian church. Two of the sons, Luther and Courtland, settled on Bayou Sarah, then West Florida, where they resided for upwards of fifty years. Their families became the most wealthy and respectable in that community.

"In September, 1805, Bishop Benjamin Moore, of the Protestant Episcopal Church, New York, received a letter from James M. Bradford, James C. Williamson, and Edward Livingston, dated New Orleans, August 12, 1805, requesting him to send them a minister of the gospel, of the Protestant Episcopal denomination, adding, 'It is to be recollected, that his supporters are not only of his own persuasion, but also Presbyterians, Catholics, etc.' Bishop Moore recommended the Rev. Philander Chase, rector of the church of Poughkeepsie, N. Y., who consented to go, and arrived in New Orleans on the 13th of November. An act of incorporation had been obtained on the 16th of November, and a vestry organized, consisting of the following persons: J. B. Provost, D. A. Hall, Benjamin Morgan, Joseph Saul, William Kenney, Joseph McNiel, George T. Ross, Charles Norwood, Andrew Burk, R. D. Shepherd, Richard Relf, Ed. Livingston, J. McDonough, T. P. Sanderson, and A. R. Ellery.

"On Sunday, November 17, 1805, at 11 A.M., the Rev. Philander Chase preached the first Protestant sermon ever delivered in New Orleans or Louisiana; and on Wednesday a vote of thanks was voted by the vestry to Mr. Chase, for his readiness and zeal in tendering his services, proffering him a salary of $2,000 per annum, and a house, or nearly $3,000 yearly in lieu of it, which he accepted, as their rector, and remained until the autumn of 1811, when he returned to the North, and became rector of Christ Church, Hartford, Connecticut.

"In 1815, soon after the close of the war with England, Mr. James Hull (said to have been a licentiate of the Presbyterian Church, Ireland) came to New Orleans from Georgia, and after preaching for a few months to the Protestant congregation, went to New York, and, unexpectedly to many of the people, received ordination from the Episcopal Bishop; returned to New Orleans, and became rector of the Episcopal church, Alfred Hennan, Esq., becoming one of the vestry. Mr. Hull ended his days in New Orleans.

"On the 30th of December, 1817, the Rev. Elias Cornelius, on an agency to the southwestern Indians, for the American Board of Commissioners for Foreign Missions, arrived in New Orleans; and much to the gratification and delight of the Protestant worshipers, preached several times, while awaiting the arrival of the Rev. Sylvester Larned, who came on the 22d of January, 1818. The people were charmed with Mr. Larned's eloquence and powers; and, on the 9th of February, held a meeting to take measures for the erection of a second Protestant house of worship for his accommodation, and subscribed $6,200 for that object; and soon after increased it to $40,000, and extended to him a call to become their pastor, with a salary of $4,000 per annum, which he accepted. The church edifice was erected the following year (1819), and on the 31st of August, 1820, Mr. Larned died of yellow fever." (See Rev. R. R. Gurley's *Life of Sylvester Larned.*)

NOTE.—In the following articles I am materially indebted to the Rev. Henry McDonald, now of Texas, who has placed at my disposal the following reminiscences of the early times in Mississippi. From materials so ample, from a source so authentic, from an old friend so accurate and so perfectly reliable, I have condensed into a small space the richest portion of the early history of the South-west.

BEGINNINGS OF

PRESBYTERIANISM IN MISSISSIPPI.

THE religious history of the Southwest received a coloring from its civil and political history. In 1682 La Salle, the able French commandant of Fort Frontenac, situated on Lake Ontario, below the site of the modern city of Buffalo, with thirty-five other Frenchmen—one of them was a Jesuit priest and missionary—penetrated from that fort to the head waters of Illinois River. He descended the river to its confluence with the Mississippi, and the Mississippi to its confluence with the Gulf of Mexico; and was the first white man who ever beheld the mouth of the "Great Father of Waters." At this point he erected a column, on which he erected the arms of France and the Cross. Before this cross he performed solemn religious ceremonies, and in the name of France and the Pope took formal possession of the country, on both sides of the river, from the top of the Alleghany to the Pacific Ocean. The French occupation established the Church of Rome in this magnificent empire, and excluded from it the Protestant worship. The preaching of the Gospel was probably not attempted. As the result of the war which grew out of the conflicting boundaries of the French and British colonies, in which the world became involved in 1763, France ceded to Great Britain, Canada and all the countries east of the Mississippi, except the Island of New Orleans; and Spain ceded to Great Britain, Florida. Great Britain erected Florida into two provinces, under the names of East and West

Florida, and attached the section known as the Natchez country to West Florida. Religious liberty was established under British rule, and gratuitous grants of land were made to settlers. This benign policy drew to the Natchez country some valuable citizens. Among them was the Rev. Samuel Swayze, who, with his brother, Richard Swayze, and a number of emigrant families, mostly his married children and relations, in 1773 emigrated from New Jersey and settled on the Homochitto River, on the Ogden grant, and near what afterwards was called the town of Kingston. It became known as the "Jersey settlement." The Rev. Samuel Swayze had been a Congregational minister in New Jersey for many years, and most of his children and relatives had been members of his church in that State. Soon after their arrival in their new homes in the wilderness, he organized them into a Congregational church. It was the first church of any Protestant denomination ever organized in the Southwest, and Mr. Swayze was the first Protestant minister. The names of these colonists were: Swayze, Farrar, Fowler, Coleman, Calender, Corey, King, Douglas, Lucy, Hopkins, Griffing, etc. Their descendants constitute numerous and influential families in Louisiana, Mississippi, Arkansas, and Texas; and they have contributed largely in shaping the destiny of the Methodist, Presbyterian, and Baptist Churches in these great States. The old graveyard is still seen in Kingston, and in it is the grave of the father of Rev. Timothy Dwight, D. D. He and his brother-in-law, General Lyman, lost their title-deeds to all that rich body of land embracing the city of Natchez and the surrounding region.

One result of the American revolutionary war was, that Great Britain ceded to Spain East and West Florida. The Natchez country was made a Spanish province, and continued under Spanish rule for eighteen years. This event closed the Southwest against the preaching of the Gospel. Protestant worship was strictly forbidden. The Congregational Church in Jersey settlement, southwest of Natchez, was broken up, and never re-organized. Rev. Samuel Swayze and wife died eleven years after coming to the country, and were buried on the Bluff, near Fort Rosalie, where the entire graveyard was precipitated into the river. Persons detected in religious worship not in conformity with the Catholic Church were now cast into the Natchez prison. Protestant marriages were forbidden. As a condition of the release of Protestant prisoners, they were threatened, on renewal of their offense, to be sent as slaves to the mines of Mexico. Thrilling scenes occurred; of worship, with sentinels picketed out to give notice of the approach of executioners of the law; and traditions have been handed down among the descendants of old families, as precious memorials of a pious and heroic ancestry. Among the faithful and true Christian men who suffered imprisonment for holding religious meetings, were John Bolls, a ruling elder in the Presbyterian church, and the Rev. Richard Curtis, a Baptist preacher.

But the Head of the Church had designed not to keep the Southwest long closed against the progress of the Gospel. During the night of the 29th of March, 1798, the Spanish governor, with the troops under his command, secretly evacuated Fort Rosalie and departed for New Orleans; and early the next morning the American flag was raised, and American jurisdiction proclaimed. This act conferred religious liberty on the province. Soon after, the Rev. Mr. Curtis, who had suffered imprisonment for preaching the Gospel, organized a Baptist Church, called Salem. It was the first church organized under the American rule. It was located on the south branch of Coles's Creek, ten miles from the present site of the town of Fayette, in Jefferson County. The house of worship has disappeared, but the graveyard is preserved, and on the gravestones are inscribed the names of many pioneers of religion and influence. At the date of the organization of this church Mr. Curtis was the only minister of any Protestant denomination in the territory. He died in 1818, at an advanced age, in Amite County, Mississippi.

The next minister of the Gospel who arrived in the province was the Rev. Tobias Gibson, who arrived in April, 1799, and in 1800 organized a Methodist Church at Washington, the seat of the territorial government, six miles east of Natchez. In 1804 he died, and was buried near Warrenton, below Vicksburg, and a suitable monument marked his grave. Who can enumerate the descendants of the Gibsons?

The Presbyterian Church was the next to enter the field. It was by a missionary enterprise of the Synod of North Carolina, the jurisdiction of which extended at that time over the States of North Carolina, South Carolina, and Georgia. But the charter granted by the British government included within Georgia all the territory west of the present limits of that State to the Mississippi River, constituting the present States of Alabama and Mississippi. After Georgia, in 1803, relinquished this territory to the Federal government, the Synod of Carolina continued for many years to be the nearest Presbyterial jurisdiction. On the establishment of American civil authority over the Mississippi Territory, in 1798, it naturally came under the ecclesiastical jurisdiction of the Synod of Carolina; and that Synod immediately adopted efficient measures to send the Gospel and plant the Church in it.

The mode of conducting domestic missions at that day seems to have been derived from the Kirk of Scotland, under the idea that it was the development of the divinely-appointed system of church government, without any addition of human inventions. It was practiced by the Presbyterian Church from its earliest planting on the American continent, and continued to be practiced for many years, until it was modified, and to some extent superseded, by innovations derived from the plan of union with the Congregational Church, in the form of voluntary societies and ecclesiastical boards. The old plan was for the Church to conduct her missions through the immediate agency of her own divinely ordained courts, which appointed the missionaries, and provided for their support.

REV. JAMES SMYLIE.

THE second Presbyterian minister who settled permanently in the Southwest, was Rev. James Smylie. He was born in North Carolina, of highland Scotch parentage, about the year 1780. He received his classical and theological education at Guildford, under the Rev. Dr. Caldwell; and was licensed and ordained by the Orange Presbytery. In 1805, soon after he was ordained, he was sent by the Synod of North Carolina, as a missionary, to the Territory of Mississippi. He settled at Washington, the capital of the Territory, and took charge of the church gathered by the missionary who preceded him. In 1811 Mr. Smylie removed to Amite County, and engaged actively in the work of the ministry in that region. He organized a number of churches in that section of Mississippi and the contiguous parishes of Louisiana. He planted Christianity and Presbyterianism over a wide extent of country, and greatly elevated the standard of education. Many of his scholars became leading men. In 1814 he traveled on horseback, through the Choctaw and Chicasaw nations, to Tennessee, to attend a meeting of the West Tennessee Presbytery, in order to get that Presbytery to petition the Synod of Kentucky for the creation of a new Presbytery for the Southwest. The Synod, at their sessions in 1815, granted the petition, and erected the new Presbytery of Mississippi, with jurisdiction from Perdido indefinitely westward. Their first act, after organizing, was to pass a vote of thanks to Mr. Smylie for procuring the organization. Their second act was to elect him as their stated clerk, which office he filled with great acceptance, until the division of the body into the three Presbyteries of Mississippi, Clinton, and Amite, and he fell into the bounds of the latter body.

When the storm of abolitionism arose, and swept with the violence of a hurricane over the country, he was one of the first men to oppose it. He prepared a sermon giving the Scriptural views on the subject, and preached it extensively over the country. In 1836 the Presbytery of Chilicothe addressed a violent abolition letter to the Presbytery of Mississippi. This letter Mr. Smylie answered, and published his answer in a pamphlet. The pamphlet was extensively circulated, and the whole question of domestic slavery was universally agitated, and influenced the legislation of the country. It was regarded as a sort of text-book on the subject, and exerted a large influence in shaping the subsequent course of the South both in Church and State.

In his old age he devoted his time exclusively to the instruction of the negroes. He collected large congregations of them. In addition to his preaching to them, and expounding to them the Holy Scriptures, he taught them the larger and shorter catechisms, and large classes of them could repeat the whole of these formularies by memory. He was earnest and bold in preaching before his brethren in the ministry, and the masters and owners of negroes, the paramount duty of imparting to them religious instruction. He had an acute and original mind, and was a close observer and careful thinker. He was an accurate Latin and Greek scholar, a profound theologian, and a thorough Calvinist. His sermons were remarkable for their great simplicity and perspicuity, and were always listened to with attention and interest. He was thoroughly versed in all the business of the Church; and in ecclesiastical courts his views generally prevailed. In private life he was remarkable for candor, integrity, and truth. He had wonderful power in conciliating and pleasing those with whom he had intercourse, and his great business habits gave him great weight of character. His word, on any subject, was regarded as settling the question. He was thrice married, and left one child by each marriage—a daughter and two sons—all of whom are married, and have large families. He died in 1853, aged seventy-three years. He left many valuable manuscripts behind him, but, by a strange misunderstanding among his family and friends, nothing has ever yet seen the light, excepting "Smylie on Slavery."

The third Presbyterian minister who permanently settled in the Southwest was the Rev. Jacob Rickhow, who was born in 1768, on Staten Island, N. Y. His parents were the earliest settlers of the place; his father of a Dutch, and his mother of an English family. He was often heard to speak of the impression made on his mind, when only eight years old, by witnessing a skirmish between some British and American troops, at Perth Amboy. He had not the advantage of a collegiate or classical education. When he was between twenty-one and twenty-four years of age he began to preach in connection with the Methodist Episcopal Church, and was ordained to the work of the ministry by Bishop Asbury. In 1808 he and another minister were received into the Presbytery of New Brunswick. Arriving in Natchez in June following, he there opened a school, and preached to a little flock of Presbyterians. In 1801 he one day met, in Natchez, with Mr. Dugald Torrey, who invited him to send an appointment to the Scotch settlement of Presbyterians in the adjoining county of Jefferson. He complied with the request, and kept up a stated monthly appointment in connection with his Natches labors, some thirty miles distant. A temporary bush arbor was erected, which was soon supplanted by a log house of worship. A considerable congregation was collected, a ruling elder elected, and the church was named Ebenezer, by which it is called to this day. In 1814 he removed to a farm in the vicinity of Port Gibson, where he remained until the death of his wife, which occurred but a few years before his own death. In 1817 he was appointed, by the General Assembly, itinerant missionary to Amite County and the neighboring parishes of Louisiana. At a later day he became the great missionary to the Piny Woods counties of Eastern Mississippi, in the region of Pearl River. Then you saw him in all his glory. In the hot days of August, he was mounted on his gray mare, with solemn pace traversing those long stretches through the piny woods, and with his reproving frown, curbing those young blades that accompanied him, Chamberlain, Helme, Butler, and Hutchison! He had the true spirit of a pioneer preacher. The Piny Woods churches seemed to belong to him. No sacramental meeting, or baptism of a child, seemed to be right without his presence. He was indefatigable in his long journeys on horseback, and in his old age enduring the fatigue of all weathers and all seasons for the glorious privilege of preaching the Gospel. But he had marked peculiarities. He was a great stickler for English grammar, accurate in the use of words, and in precise conformity to dates. He would never forget a *lapsus linguæ* dropped by a young brother. Having been a sailor in his youth, he contended, with great warmth, that there was no such things as "equinoctial storms." Being called upon to ask a blessing over a Sabbath dinner, he refused, by asserting "that this food was cooked on Sunday." Because of his constant and inseparable intimacy with his venerable brother, Rev. W. Montgomery, Dr. George Potts called them the "Siamese Twins." After the death of his wife he removed to Mississippi City, where he resided with his son-in-law, and died November 23, 1855, at the advanced age of 87 years.

In a letter to his intimate friend, Rev. Dr. Butler, of Port Gibson, dated October 30, about three weeks before his death, and doubtless the last words he ever wrote, he said: "I wish and desire, like Paul, in whatever state I am, therewith to be content. I do not despond. I remember what the Psalmist says, 'I have been young and now am old, yet I have not seen the righteous forsaken, or his seed begging bread.' I do not claim to be righteous, only as I hope to stand justified by the imputed righteousness of Christ. I wish to be entirely conformed to the Divine will.

BEGINNINGS OF

PRESBYTERIANISM IN THE SOUTHWEST.

The modern facilities for travel were unknown at the beginning of the present century. The only mode of travel was on horseback. The route was first to Nashville, and from that place to Natchez, through the nations of the Shawnee, Cherokee, Chickasaws, and Choctaw Indians, over a road known as "The Natchez Trace"—the only road known in the country. It was infested by a numerous band of robbers, under the celebrated Mason; and the stories of Mason and the Harpes, handed down by tradition, were as romantic as the adventures of Robin Hood. It was not unusual for travelers on the road to be killed and robbed. So common were these deeds of violence, that to see a human body covered with blood by the roadside, the pockets and saddle-bags rifled, gave no surprise; and such were the perils of that long journey through the wilderness, that travelers always set out well armed, prepared to meet the most dangerous emergencies. The thought of adventuring on it under other conditions never occurred to the most daring men. But these missionaries were prompted by motives different from other travelers. Their motives were not to become owners of any of those large tracts of fertile land which were thrown open to ordinary adventurers. They set out on that road without carnal weapons or defensive armor, save an unwavering faith in their Divine leader, and the protection of an overruling Providence. They traveled on horseback, with an extra horse as a pack-horse, on which they carried their provisions and camp-fixtures. They cooked their own provisions, camped out at night, and forded the rivers and swollen streams. When they pitched their tents at nightfall, and sat round their blazing fire, the lonely forests rung with their hymns of lofty cheer.

In the northern part of the present State of Mississippi, near the site of the modern town of Pontotoc, which was then occupied by the Chickasaw Indians, they called and spent the night at the mission station, which three years before Rev. Joseph Bullen had established among the Indians. To a late hour in the night they sat up, and talked over their plans for extending the Redeemer's kingdom in the great South. Mr. Samuel Bullen, recently deceased, near Fayette, Mississippi, at an advanced age, related this visit of the missionaries to his venerable father as one of the most pleasing reminiscences of his life. He was then a boy. Soon after leaving Nashville they fell in company with some men who were driving horses to the South for some families who had gone down the river in boats. These travelers contributed their company and security, but were not well supplied with provisions, supposing that they could easily purchase all they might need from the Indians. But the Indians at that season had mostly gone west of the Mississippi, on their fall hunt. Consequently the travelers were nearly reduced to starvation. The missionaries shared their provisions with them. Their stock of provisions became exhausted, and at last all was gone except a little meal, which was equally divided. This they mixed with a little water, and ate with thankful hearts, calling it "gruel." At one time they caught a racoon, which they ate without salt or condiments, giving God the glory. They pressed forward night and day, as fast as their horses could carry them, in the hope of relief. On the morning of December 4, 1800, about two o'clock, they drew near to a dwelling on Big Black River. The first intimation they had of their proximity to a human habitation was the crowing of a cock, which sounded in their ears like music. They hastened to the house, and without ceremony aroused the inmates, alleging starvation as their apology. They were kindly received, and bacon, corn-bread, and coffee were furnished them. Rev. William Montgomery, forty years after, in referring to this night's adventure, remarked, "It was a night never to be forgotten." "But light cometh in the morning."

At Big Black the missionaries established a preaching station; a few miles farther south, they established another station at Grindstone Ford; a few miles farther south, they established another at Clark's Creek. The first town they reached was Port Gibson. In this town they did not find a single member of the Presbyterian Church, and not a professor of any other denomination. But they met with an intelligent and hospitable people, who treated them with great kindness. A few hours before their arrival, Mrs. Gibson, the wife of the original settler whose name was given to the town, had died. At the request of Mr. Gibson, Mr. Montgomery preached the funeral sermon. It was the first sermon of any description ever preached in the town, unless some one may have previously heard Rev. John Gibson or Rev. Mr. Curtis.

A few miles southwest of the town, they found many Presbyterian families, exceedingly anxious for religious privileges. Here the people united and built a log church, and called it Bayou Pierre church. They continued their course south, along the Natchez trace, until they crossed Coles's Creek. Here they found a small town, called Uniontown, to which they were attracted by the name of Montgomery, where they found two brothers of that name, Samuel and Alexander Montgomery, who had emigrated to that vicinity from Kentucky, and originally from Georgia. They were planters of influence. Alexander Montgomery had been the speaker of the first territorial legislature of Mississippi. They were Presbyterians, and found others, anxious, with them, to secure religious privileges. Among their neighbors, there were seven families, who had emigrated from New Jersey with Rev. Samuel Swayze, and had united with him in forming the church at Kingston. After this church had been broken up by the Spaniards, these families had settled at Uniontown. Their names were Jeremiah Coleman, Israel Coleman, Ephraim Coleman, John Griffing, Alexander Callender, Archibald Douglass and Stephen Douglass.

A few miles distant was Felix Hughes, an intelligent Irishman of Episcopal education, whose wife had been a devout member of the Presbyterian Church in North Carolina. Sufficiently near to unite with them, was the renowned John Bolls, of blessed memory, and who shall often appear in this volume, who, under the Spanish rule, had braved the tyrants' wrath in behalf of religion, and suffered imprisonment for holding prayer-meetings. He had been a ruling elder of Hopewell church, in South Carolina, before the Revolutionary War, was in the Mecklenburg Convention when the first Declaration of Independence was adopted, had served as a soldier in the Revolutionary army, was a man of devout piety and heroic courage, and helped to lay the foundation of many churches in Mississippi.

Three years after, in 1804, the foregoing named families were organized into the first Presbyterian church ever organized in the Southwest, with Alexander Montgomery, John Bolls, Alexander Callender, and

John Griffing as ruling elders. In 1817, John Alesworth, Daniel Huey and Joseph Parmalee were added to the session. The church has never become extinct, but exists at this time, in an enlarged form, and in a contiguous locality, under another name. "It shall be said of this man and of that man, he was born there." A true narrative of the first Presbyterian church ever organized in the great Southwest will relate the number and names of the men who have become eminent in church and State, and who have planted the church in other sections, received in this church and under the influence it diffused, that moral training, which made them blessings to their country. The three missionaries, however, did not organize this church. They collected these families into a congregation, and formed the nucleus for a future church. These persons united and built a log house of worship on land belonging to Alexander Callender, and called it Callender's meeting-house. It was located near the southern bank of Coles's Creek, in sight of the road leading from Port Gibson to Natchez, in a cluster of beautiful trees, on land which now belongs to Wade Harrison. The house of worship has long since gone to decay; but the graveyard is sacredly preserved, and on the rough gravestones are engraved precious names, which are doubtless written in the book of life, and ought to be held in lasting remembrance by all who love the founders of Southern Presbyterianism.

The missionaries continued their course south, along the Natchez trace. The next point which they reached was Washington, the capital of the territory. Here they found the state of things still more interesting. In the vicinity were many Presbyterian families of wealth, intelligence and high social position, to whom they proposed to establish a place of worship.

The next point which they reached was Natchez, and there they found only one Presbyterian family. But that family was that of John Henderson, a name which has become identified with the Natchez church down to the present time, and has proved a tower of strength to the cause of Christ. In the vicinity of Natchez, they found some of the most eminent families who once belonged to Mr. Swayze's congregation, but dispersed by the Spanish authorities. Holding the same standard of doctrinal faith with the Presbyterian church, they readily co-operated with the missionaries. South of this point, they next reached Pinckneyville, not far from the boundary line of the Territory, as had been laid down by Andrew Ellicott, the surveyor, and whose book is now almost entirely gone out of print. There were nine preaching stations, which they established in Big Black, Grindstone Ford, Clark's Creek, Bayou Pierre, Callender's meeting-house, Washington, Natchez, Jersey settlement, and Pinckneyville. It has never been the custom or policy of the Presbyterian Church to organize churches hastily, or without prospects of permanence. Their plan seems to have been to explore the country, to hunt up the members of the church, who were scattered abroad like sheep without a shepherd, and, by the aid of leading members of the new communities, to establish, at eligible points, preaching stations and nuclei of future churches. Of the nine which they established, five were subsequently organized into churches, all of which exist at this time, in the original locations or in places contiguous, where greater convenience is secured for the mass of the community. During the seventy years which have elapsed since these noble missionaries collected the scattered sheep in this vast wilderness, these congregations have passed through great changes—have had their joys and sorrows. They have steadily poured their saving influences over the communities where they have been located, and sent forth ten thousand streams of salvation, to gladden the hearts of millions then unborn. These five original churches constituted the germ of the first Presbytery which, in 1816, was organized at Pine Ridge, and extended from Perdido river indefinitely westward, and at this day embrace several entire synods.

REV. W. MONTGOMERY.

The fourth permanent Presbyterian minister, who permanently settled in the South, the Rev. William Montgomery, was born at Shippensburg, Pa., in 1768. In early youth, his father removed to South Carolina; and some say that he graduated at the Chapel Hill University. He was an admirable classical scholar, and, late in life, his friend Horace was his *vade mecum.* He took a thorough course in theological studies, and was licensed and ordained in North Carolina. Mr. Huey, who heard him preach in 1810, describes him at that time, as quite young in personal appearance, handsome to a fault, dignified, candid and kind, an example in manners, a stranger to everything hidden, and singularly animated and fluent in speech. He commenced preaching by writing his sermon in full, keeping his manuscript before him in the delivery. At an early day in his ministry, he changed his method, and preached without notes. In his best days, he was a preacher of great popularity, and drew large audiences. In the year 1800, the Synod of Carolina selected him, in connection with Rev. James Hall and Rev. James Bowman, as missionaries to the new territory of Mississippi, then just coming under American jurisdiction. The Rev. Dr. Ashbel Green, in his history of the missions of the Presbyterian Church, represents the preeminent success of these young missionaries. They planted the germ of the first Presbyterian churches in the Southwest, which, in 1816, were formed into the Presbytery of Mississippi, and at one time embraced the present Synods of Alabama, Mississippi, Memphis, Arkansas and Texas. When this mission was completed, Mr. Montgomery returned to Georgia, and settled as pastor of the church of Lexington, in that State. Soon after his settlement at that place, he was united in marriage to Miss Lane, niece of General Joseph Lane, who, in 1860, was the candidate for the vice-presidency of the United States, on the ticket with John C. Breckenridge for the presidency. It was during his ministry in that place, that the great awakening and revival of religion prevailed over that section, attended with the extraordinary nervous convulsions, called the "jerks." In this great revival, he was one of the most active and useful laborers. At first he was suspicious of these strange physical phenomena. But at last he became convinced of their adaptedness to the times, and the people. In 1810, he once more visited Mississippi, with the view of finding a permanent field of labor. In 1811, he removed, with his family, to Washington, the territorial capital, and became President of Jefferson College, at that place. But he soon resigned this position, that he might devote all his time to the work of the ministry. He was pastor of Pine Ridge church, in connection with other fields of labor. Soon after his arrival, in 1811, one day in Natchez, he was introduced to a stranger, Mr. Dugald Torrey, who became his friend for life. At his request, he sent an appointment to Ebenezer church, which Rev. Jacob Rickhow a short time previously had organized in the Scotch settlement, in the adjoining county of Jefferson. This appointment resulted in a call to become pastor of the two churches, of Ebenezer and Union, which he accepted, in connection with his charge at Pine Ridge church. Subsequently, by the aid of Mr. Torrey, he purchased a section of land, on which he raised a large family, and resided during the remainder of his life. He was pastor of Ebenezer and Union churches for thirty-seven years, from 1811 to 1848, for some years in connection with Pine Ridge and Harmony church. But he finally gave up all other work, and devoted his time alternately to these two fields, and built them up to be finally the largest churches in the Synod. Every year there were considerable accessions to their memberships. On one occasion, in 1852, the writer (J. R. H.) witnessed an accession of thirty members to Union church. A spirit of devout piety always prevailed. Father Montgomery was scrupulous to meet all his appointments; and, during his long ministry in this field, he failed only to meet two appointments, one failure caused by the death of his wife, the other, by the death of a son. The inclemencies of the weather he never viewed as a sufficient excuse for absence. Hence, large congregations often attended through the rain, knowing that Mr. Montgomery would be sure to be there. His sermons were more didactic and instructive than emotional. During some periods of his ministry, *flush times* prevailed in the country, and opportunities for making fortunes even seized some of the clergy. But these temptations had no effect upon him. A good or bad season of crops affected him equally, and his life was the same under all circumstances. After his death, one of his neighbors remarked that his life was like the spring of water which gushed from a hill near his door, and which poured forth its clear stream through all seasons of the year, and through all years alike. Through all his life, his wants were well supplied, and when he died, he bequeathed considerable property to his children. He was never suspected by any one of unfair dealing, or of anything sinister or hidden. He was candid, honest and sincere. In his social intercourse, he was emphatically genial, with large stores of humorous anecdotes, collected in a long lifetime, which he could tell well. In old age, he was a great favorite with the young, and over a wide extent of country he exerted a great influence. One cause which contributed to this widespread influence, arose from the fact, that the older members of these churches were born in the Highlands of Scotland, and many others were of Scotch extraction, emigrants from North Carolina. But the standard of piety among them was elevated. They loved their pastor, and by their prayers and personal influence, held up his hands. This mutual affection was reciprocal, and closed only with the grave. At the time of his death, a living generation had grown up under his influence. He had baptized most of them in infancy, united most of their parents in marriage, and buried their dead. His last illness was received in that place and occupation where every faithful servant of Christ would love to be found. It was in the pulpit, preaching the Gospel. He rode to church, fifteen miles, in the rain, and preached in damp clothes. He took cold, which induced pneumonia. The Rev. Henry McDonald preached his funeral sermon to a large congregation, and he was laid to rest beside his wife, who had preceded him several years. He died in 1848, was eighty years of age, and had been in the ministry fifty years He left two daughters and five sons, one of whom is Rev. Samuel Montgomery. One son, William, who was a candidate for the ministry, died while a member of the senior class at Oakland College, a few weeks before he graduated. "I was with him at the time," writes Mr. McDonald, "though at that time I was not a professor of religion.

The thought of an early death, so young, so sudden, so different from all human expectations and prospects, had rather a depressing effect upon his mind at first. But this depression was only momentary, and was succeeded by the most intense joy. He conversed with all the students, told them his views and feelings, and fervently exhorted them to become Christians. This death-bed scene diffused deep religious convictions over all the students of the college, and was one of the circumstances which brought a number of the students into the Christian ministry. It is not improbable that the sermons which young Montgomery preached from his death-bed were attended by greater results than the long ministry of many living preachers.

REV. ZEBULON BUTLER, D. D.

The Rev. Dr. Butler was born in Wilkesbarre, in Wyoming Valley, Pennsylvania, on September 27, 1803. His father was an officer in the revolutionary army under Washington. The name of his mother was Lord. His brother, Chester Butler, was a member of Congress. They were an Episcopal family of intelligence, refinement, and wealth. Dr. Butler was educated at Princeton College, and graduated in 1822. In college he was regarded as a good scholar, of great amiability, and of great popularity among the students. In the early part of his collegiate course he was careless of religion, full of humor, always ready for amusement, mingling with the gay and wild students, and engaging in all their sports. But in his senior year a revival of religion prevailed in the college, of which he became a subject, and which changed the whole current of his life. After he graduated he took charge of an academy in his native town, and, in pursuance of a long-cherished plan, commenced the study of medicine. But, on reflection, he found that his public profession of religion involved a surrender of his plans and of himself to the Lord Jesus Christ, and left him no liberty to follow the promptings of worldly interest or human ambition. He lifted up his eyes and saw the fields white unto the harvest, and the laborers few. Such thoughts deeply impressed him, and led him to select a course of action differing from the wishes of his friends and the great purposes of his life. After an earnest inquiry as to what the Lord would have him to do, all doubts were removed from his mind, and he submissively surrendered himself to the convictions of a Divine call to the ministry. Under the force of this grand conviction he abandoned the study of medicine, and in the fall of 1823 he entered the Theological Seminary at Princeton. During his senior year in the seminary Dr. Alexander one day placed in his hand a letter, written by some citizen of Vicksburg, Mississippi. In it was described the spiritual destitution of that place, and an earnest request was added, that some young man from the seminary should be sent to preach the Gospel to that new and growing city. This letter deeply affected Mr. Butler, and he promptly agreed to go. Soon after, he was licensed by the Presbytery; and, mounting his horse, and after encountering many adventures on the way, he traveled by land to Vicksburg. He reached that place in the fall of 1826, being twenty-three years of age, and of exceedingly youthful appearance. There was not a single house of worship in the place, and no Presbyterian organization had been attempted, and only a feeble band of Methodists had been called together under the ministry of Rev. John Lane. The only place of worship for all denominations was an upper room, the lower room being occupied as a drinking-saloon. Mr. Lane and Mr. Butler cordially fraternized, and made common cause against the kingdom of Satan. Mr. Butler soon established a stated appointment at Clinton, a flourishing town, being before the location of the State capitol at Jackson. His way to that church was through the town of Port Gibson, and the only mode of travel was by horseback. As he was riding through the streets of the town some one hailed him, and placed a letter in his hand. It contained an invitation from the citizens to preach the Gospel to them. There was a single place of worship in the town. The Methodist brethren had a small church organization. A few months after accepting the invitation of the people he organized a Presbyterian church in the Court-house, consisting of twelve members, and Mr. Alexander Armstrong was chosen ruling elder. He now commenced alternating with the people of Fayette, the new seat of government of Jefferson County; but the interest in religion among the citizens of Fort Gibson soon demanded all his time. Many influential ladies united with the church. But there were scoffers in those days, unwilling to tolerate a mere boy in breaking up their gay amusements, and changing the whole order of things. Still he persevered. He studied hard, sat up late, burned the midnight lamp, and wrote his sermons with great care. He imparted singular pathos and animation to his delivery. He had the power of saying pathetic and persuasive things. His prayers had power. His lips seemed to be touched with a live coal from God's altar. Whole congregations were often melted to tears by his addresses to the throne of grace. His youthful and exceedingly handsome personal appearance imparted great attractions to his delivery. He held prayer-meetings, established Bible-classes and Sabbath-schools, and warned the people with tears, and from house to house. An extensive revival of religion soon followed. The converts numbered persons of all classes. Among them were ladies who had been the leaders of fashion, lawyers, merchants, physicians, the old and the young, and many who had late been scoffers. The sound of the viol and the noise of mirth were soon hushed, and gave place to hymns of praise. Speedily a handsome brick church was erected, where for many succeeding years his words distilled like the dew. The neighboring churches sent for him, and many were added to the Lord. Over a wide extent of country his name became a household word, and for many long years he was regarded with unbounded confidence and affection.

The leading and primary object of the founders of Oakland College was to raise up in the Southwest a native ministry. An unknown donor contributed $25,000 to endow a theological professorship. In 1837, the Presbytery of Mississippi, who at that time controlled the college, elected Mr. Butler temporary professor, until a permanent arrangement could be made. In a short time the Rev. S. Beach Jones, of New Jersey, was elected professor. The theological professorship continued for some years, and many young men, not merely of the Presbyterian, but of other churches, entered the ministry. In the meantime numerous calls from other churches poured in on Mr. Butler. He received calls from the McCord Church of Lexington, and from the First Church of Louisville, Kentucky, and from other city churches. He declined them all with so much promptitude that it soon became understood that he conceived himself as a fixture at Gibson. To the end of his life his brethren in the ministry regarded him as "the beloved disciple." He always conceded, in all Presbyterial arrangements, a conspicuous place to his brethren; and in all appointments of Presbytery he was always the most zealous and active in laboring in poor and desolate congregations. In 1860 the old church in which he had preached so long and so successfully was taken down and supplanted by a more elegant and costly edifice, at a cost of $40,000. But into this new house he was never permitted to enter. When nearly completed, one morning he rode round the building in a carriage, and with anxious eye surveyed its exterior, but was too weak to enter, and rode sadly away. He never left his room again.

Several years of declining health were allotted to him. He was aware of his situation. Death found him with his lamp trimmed and his light burning. He spoke exultingly of his full assurance of faith, and immediate entrance into heaven. He spoke freely and fully of it to all his friends. His last words were, "Glory to God, glory to God!" He died December 23, 1860.

In 1829 he was married to Miss Mary Ann Murdoch, a lady eminently qualified to be a helpmeet to such a noble man, who went heart and soul with him in all his good works; and much of his success in the ministry was attributed to her influence. She was born in Ireland, in 1811, but in her infancy her parents emigrated to Port Gibson, where she was raised. She died October 5, 1863. They had eleven children, most of whom died young. Three sons and two daughters are still living.

EBENEZER AND UNION CHURCHES, IN MISSISSIPPI.

On April 6, 1806, two keel-boats on the Mississippi were moored at the landing at Bruinsburg, containing four emigrant Presbyterian families,—George Torrey, Dugald Torrey, Lockland Currie, and Mr. Willis.

George Torrey, Lockland Currie and Mr. Willis were born in the Highlands of Scotland, before the Revolutionary War, but had settled for some years in North Carolina. The object in mooring their boats at Bruinsburg was to obtain information from Judge Bruin respecting the new country east of Natchez. Dugald Torrey was selected to confer with Judge Bruin, who had recently been appointed Judge of the Supreme Court of the Territory. As he approached the house, he observed three gentlemen at the window, one of whom rose and came to meet him. To his joy and surprise, this gentleman proved to be his friend, the Rev. Mr. Brown, a Presbyterian minister, who came to the Territory as a missionary, from North Carolina. He had preached the day before in the neighborhood, and on that morning was on a visit to Judge Bruin, with Waterman Crane. These gentlemen conceived a warm friendship for the emigrants. By their advice, instead of descending the river to Natchez, the strangers ascended the Bayou Pierre to Port Gibson, in the vicinity of which they rented a temporary home, and made a crop. This gave them an opportunity to become acquainted with the country and make a judicious location of a permanent home. During the year, they purchased land in the eastern part of Jefferson County. The whole country east of their location, as far as the State of Georgia, was an unbroken wilderness. The settlement of these Scotch-Irish Presbyterians on the border of an unknown wilderness of public land, just having been surveyed, and offered at government price, with the right of pre-emption to actual settlers, at once attracted numerous other settlers of the same race and religion. In a few years, over one hundred Highland-Scotch Presbyterian families settled in their vicinity. Most of them spoke the Gaelic language, had been taught the Shorter

Catechism, and forms of worship and usages of the Presbyterian Church; and were persons of elevated and devout piety. Among them were families by the names of Gilcrist, Baker, Cameron, McIntyre, McLauchlin, McLaurin, Buie, Cato, Brown, Smith, Patterson, Watson, Galbreath, Smylie, Trimble, McClutchie, Farley, Curie, Wilkinson, McCormick, McMillan, McClean, Henderson, McCallum. The Southern climate has proved as favorable to the longevity of this hardy race of people as the colder climate of their native hills. And, within a few years ago, the venerable hoary heads which thronged their Sabbath services, and whose songs of praise filled the stranger with reverence and awe, formed a most impressive spectacle. The fear of the Lord, in which they and their children had been reared, proved, even for this world, the beginning of wisdom. In due time, it brought down upon them temporal as well as spiritual blessings, and many of their descendants have risen to fortune and political distinction.

DEATH

OF THE

REV. JAMES PURVIANCE, D. D.

THE Synod and Presbytery of Mississippi have lost another of that now sparse class of members who may be called the patriarchs of these bodies.

Dr. James Purviance died at his residence in Natchez, just before the hour of twelve, on the night of Wednesday, the 14th inst., 1874. For the last ten years, a chronic affection of the throat and the general exhaustions consequent upon a series of fevers, with which he was attacked in 1860, have rendered him an invalid. He has lived encamped upon the borders of the heavenly country, and, beyond an occasional effort to assist his daughters in the instruction of a female school, has had little to do with the affairs of the world. His decline was very gradual. He foresaw the fatal event—set his house in perfect order—committed himself without a misgiving into the hands of his Saviour—and, in the tranquillity of a painless sleep, passed away to his heavenly rest. His brethren could have asked for him no happier ending of life.

He was a native of Baltimore, and a member of an old and respectable family, still represented in that city by his brother, Commodore H. Y. Purviance.

His first purpose was to adopt the military profession, and, in pursuance of this, he entered the national school at West Point, where he was a class-mate of the generals R. E. Lee and Jos. E. Johnston. Abandoning this purpose, he returned to Baltimore, and entered upon the study of law, and, after a regular course of study, was admitted to the bar. Soon after this event, however, under the ministry of the late Dr. Nevins, he underwent that thorough change in his religious convictions which resulted in his profession of his faith as a Christian, and his adoption of the ministerial office as his calling. He received his theological training at Princeton. His first field of labor was Baton Rouge, Louisiana, which was then the centre of a wealthy and important district, largely infected with infidelity and interfused with a Roman Catholic population—and which, perhaps, on this account, was selected by the Missionary Board of the Church as a scene calling for the services of such gifted minds as those of Dorrance, Hutchison, and Purviance.

The reputation for comity as a gentleman, and fidelity and ability as a pastor, which the youthful evangelist acquired during his residence at Baton Rouge, led the congregation of the Carmel Church, Adams County, Mississippi, upon the withdrawal of Dr. Chase from that charge, in 1840, to extend to him a call to become their pastor. He continued at this post till 1854, when he was elected President of Oakland College. The Board of Directors, in making this choice, had not been mistaken in supposing that certain well-defined traits in the character of Dr. Purviance marked him out as a man eminently adapted to exercise an ascendency over the minds of a community of youth, and to secure to the institution under his care the benefits of good order and high-toned manners. The result fully justified their expectations, and the six years of his incumbency constitute one of the palmiest periods in the history of the college.

From this position he was constrained, from the prostration of his health, to retire in 1860, and from that time his life has been little else than a protracted struggle with disease. The ardor of his nature and the impetuosity of his will, which many who knew him only in his earlier life will recall, were beautifully tempered by Divine grace through the instrumentality of affliction, and before his departure he had become literally like a shock of corn ripened for the garner.

It is the inevitable misfortune, perhaps, of persons with as positive points of character as those which Dr. Purviance possessed, to come in collision sometimes with the opinions of their brethren; but there is no one, probably, who knew him well who will not certify that if ever there was a heart devoted to the love and maintenance of truth, it was his; and if ever there was a man since Paul's day who has verified Paul's ideal of the Christian—in the loyal soldier, the honest steward, and the single-eyed racer, and over whose grave the inscription could be written—"I have fought a good fight, I have kept the faith, I have finished my course"—it was he.

J. B. S.

REPORT OF THE COMMITTEE

APPOINTED BY

THE PRESBYTERY OF MISSISSIPPI

TO PREPARE AN OBITUARY OF THE REV. B. CHASE, D. D.

THE committee appointed to prepare an obituary of the Rev. Benjamin Chase, D. D., would report that, in compliance with the duty imposed upon them, they have compiled the following sketch of the life of this eminent and beloved father in the church, mainly from materials which his own hand has preserved in a manuscript autobiography.

Dr. Chase was born in the Township of Litchfield, New Hampshire, on the 20th of November, 1789. His ancestors came from England as early as A. D. 1635. There is satisfactory evidence that about that year, Thomas, William, and Aquila Chase—immediate descendants of Sir Robert Chase, of Cornwall—emigrated to this country, and settled, two of them, Thomas and Aquila, at Hampton, New Hampshire, and the third, William, at Yarmouth, Massachusetts. The father of Dr. Chase was Simeon Chase, the great-great-grandson of this Aquila Chase. His mother was Mary Bartlett, of Newtown, New Hampshire, which was also the birthplace of his father. Of this marriage seven children were the issue—four sons and three daughters. Benjamin was the second child, and the oldest son. His father and two brothers settled at Litchfield prior to the Revolution of 1776. They lived contiguous to each other, each possessing a good farm, and owning jointly a saw-mill and a grist-mill. The rudiments of his education were acquired at the district school. His progress in knowledge was interrupted by frequent infirmities of defective constitution, and, under the impression that he was not adapted to a student's life, he spent several of his early years in assisting his father on his farm and in his mills; and, for a considerable period, was occupied as an apprentice to a house-carpenter. In his nineteenth year, having formed the purpose to acquire a classical education, he entered the academy at Salisbury, New Hampshire; and in August, 1811, was admitted to the sophomore class in Middlebury College, Vermont. His room-mate at this institution was Reuben Post, afterwards Rev. Dr. Post, of Charleston, South Carolina; and Sylvester Larned, afterwards the first pastor of the First Presbyterian Church of New Orleans, was a member of the class in advance of him. All three of these young men became subjects of a religious awakening, which occurred while in college, and Mr. Chase was received into the Rev. Dr. Melvill's church, at Middlebury. The change in Mr. Chase was the result of convictions which dated back to an early period of his life. His mother was an eminently pious woman, who, although her death occurred when he was in his thirteenth year, had made impressions upon his mind by her instructions, which were never obliterated. His father was not a member of any church, but was a man of exemplary life, who maintained worship in his family, and was careful in the religious training of his children. Mr. Chase was graduated at college in August, 1814. His purpose, at that time, was to devote himself to teaching, as a profession. With this view, he accepted, for a brief period, a position as head of an academy in New Jersey, and subsequently was transferred to a similar position in Philadelphia, which he continued to occupy until the fall of 1817. On the 17th of December of that year he arrived in New Orleans, having made the passage thither by sea, in the hope of repairing the health of his wife. In this hope he was disappointed. The sufferer lingered till the following spring, and then died. During the winter thus spent in New Orleans, Mr. Chase was associated with Rev. Elias Cornelius, Rev. Sylvester Larned, and Rev. Jeremiah Chamberlain, in efforts to establish institutions of Protestant worship, and to promote, in various ways, the work of Christian benevolence.

After the death of his wife, he yielded to the conviction that his proper calling was the Gospel ministry, and commenced a course of theological study, under the direction of his friend, Mr. Larned, at the same time making a support for himself by teaching a school, first at New Orleans, and subsequently at St. Francisville, Louisiana. He was licensed to preach by the Presbytery of Mississippi on the 19th of November, 1820. From that time till the summer of 1823 he was, in connection with the charge of his school, engaged laboriously in the work of an evangelist, supplying the destitution of Louisiana, as far as he could reach them, at great sacrifice to his own ease, and without a dollar of pecuniary compensation.

Repeated attacks of sickness at length constrained him to seek a change of climate, and, in 1823, he left the South, with the expectation of never returning to it, being, in his own words, "only the wreck of a man, with sight impaired, teeth loose, and jaws stiffened (from salivation), and a cripple, walking with a crutch and staff."

During his sojourn in New England, and under the impression that his stay there was to be permanent, he requested ordination from a Congregational body—the

"Association of the Western District of New Haven County, Connecticut,"—and was by them ordained on the 17th of August, 1824.

In taking this step, he followed the counsel of the Rev. Gardiner Spring, D. D., of New York, who was present, and preached the sermon on the occasion of his ordination.

In the fall of that year, having been solicited to return to his old field of labor, he accepted a commission from the General Assembly's Board of Missions, and arrived in Natchez in the latter part of December.

On Christmas-day he preached at the Carmel Church, Second Creek, where a house of worship had been erected, and a church, consisting of fifteen or sixteen members, had been organized the year before.

Establishing himself at Pinkneyville, he spent the winter in preaching at a number of points in Louisiana and Mississippi which could be reached from the centre. At the spring meeting of Mississippi Presbytery, in 1825, he was received as a member of that body, the vote, however, being accompanied with a minute, expressive of the disapprobation of the Presbytery of the mode in which his ordination had been obtained, and requiring him formally to adopt the Confession of Faith and Form of Government of the Presbyterian Church.

In the year 1828, he was married to Mrs. Anna W. Smith, daughter of the late John Henderson, of Natchez, a lady eminently gifted with intelligence and piety, with whom he maintained the happiest relations, till her sudden death, in 1845, deprived him of her precious companionship.

Mrs. Smith was the owner of a residence and plantation in the Second Creek neighborhood, ten miles south of Natchez, known as Mantua; and Providence, in leading Mr. Chase into this matrimonial connection, furnished him, for the first time in his life, with the blessing of a home. In becoming a resident at "Mantua," however, he took care to have it understood, as one of the preliminaries of his marriage, that he was not, in his own language, to marry the plantation, in such a sense that the minister of the Gospel should ever become absorbed in the planter. Charge of the property was intrusted to a brother-in-law, who continued to manage it, until, after the lapse of many years, ill health forced Mr. Chase to resign the active work of the ministry.

In July, 1828, he accepted an engagement to supply the Carmel Church, in the neighborhood of his residence. Three congregations were included in this church, that of "Carmel," that of the "Old Court-house," and that of "Cold Springs." To these were added the church at Pine Ridge, and several intermediate congregations, between which and the Carmel Church Mr. Chase divided his time. It was his custom, in filling his appointments, to ride forty miles and preach three times on a Sabbath.

In 1830, he enlisted zealously in the work of supplying destitute regions of the Southwest with the Holy Scriptures. As an agent of the Mississippi Bible Society, he traversed one-half of Adams County, furnishing personally a copy of the word of God to the families who were found without it. The interest awakened in his mind by the facts disclosed by this excursion led him to devote himself to the work of circulating the Scriptures on a larger scale; and, for the next ten years, under commissions from the American Bible Association or the State societies of Louisiana and Mississippi, he was engaged in a series of labors, involving an immense exposure and toil, by means of which the whole territory of Mississippi, Louisiana, and such parts of

Arkansas and Texas as were accessible, were visited and supplied with copies of the Bible. The difficulties and perils connected with this enterprise were enough to make it heroic, and the Providence of God, which carried Mr. Chase successfully through it, was as marked as was the zeal for God which prompted him to undertake it.

The effect of the heavy tax upon his physical resources, to which he had thus subjected himself, became apparent in the autumn of 1840, when he was attacked with a bronchial affection, which involved the loss of his voice, and, for a time, threatened to communicate itself to the lungs. During the summer of 1841, he visited Europe, with material advantage to his general health, but with no relief to his organic infirmity. From this he never recovered. Although able to speak and pray sometimes at an ecclesiastical or social meeting, he was constrained to withdraw from the duties of the pulpit.

His interest in the affairs of the church, however, suffered no abatement, and he continued with almost invariable regularity, to attend the meetings of Presbytery and Synod, and occasionally represented his Presbytery in the General Assembly. As a member of several successive committees, to whom this work was intrusted, he took a prominent part in the supervision of the General Assembly's schemes of Domestic Missions and Education in the Southwest.

A great part of his attention, during the latter years of his life, was given to the fostering of Oakland College.

He had been the chairman of a committee which had been appointed by the Presbytery of Mississippi, to consider the subject of founding an institution of learning under the auspices of that body, and, at the meeting of Presbytery at Bethel Church, Claiborne County, in

January, 1830, presented an able report, which closed with a resolution "that it is expedient to establish an institution of learning now within our bounds, which, when complete, shall embrace the usual branches of science and literature taught in the colleges of our country, together with a preparatory English grammar-school, and a theological professorship seminary." This resolution was adopted; and, a few months afterwards, was carried into effect by the opening of Oakland College, under the presidency of Rev. Jeremiah Chamberlain, D. D., at its present site, in the neighborhood of Bethel Church.

Dr. Chase was a liberal patron of the infant institution, and continued to serve its interest, in the capacity of director or trustee, till near the end of his life. During the latter part of the year 1851, after the death of Dr. Chamberlain, he was its acting President until the inauguration of Rev. R. L. Stanton, D. D., as regular President.

A characteristic monument of his devotion to the institution is to be found in the Chase cabinet—a collection of specimens of mineralogy and natural history, which, in the indulgence of his own private taste, he had made, and which he had presented to the college. The value of this collection he estimated at $5,000. Another expression of his interest in the cause of education appears in the fact that, in 1851, he gratuitously conveyed to the Trustees of Austin College, Texas, through the Rev. Daniel Baker, D.D., then President of that institution, a tract of land in Texas, of which he was possessed, of 5,000 acres.

In the year 1846, in order to obtain better facilities for the education of his children, then consisting of two daughters and three sons, Dr. Chase moved from his home at Mantua to a residence at Natchez.

Mantua had grown into a sylvan Paradise under his tasteful culture during eighteen years of his occupancy. The grounds were adorned with plants and trees, which he had brought from the regions he traversed during his missionary wanderings. His cabinets were stored with fossils, minerals, and relics of the aborigines of the country; a valuable library enriched his shelves; and, adjoining his dwelling, an extensive park had been enclosed, beautified with terraces and avenues, and stocked with a herd of deer. The charm of the place, however, was always the concord and benignity which reigned within doors, and the warm, Christian hospitality which was ever ready to afford shelter to the needy, and give a welcome to the friend.

The paternal sympathies of Dr. Chase were unusually strong. He had endured hardness himself, and could feel for those who, as was the case with most of the ministry in this comparatively frontier part of the country, were actually enduring it. His benefactions were constant, liberal. The distressed brother never failed to find solace in the amenities of his roof, and to carry away from his presence invigoration from his kind words and deeds.

On one occasion he made a fatiguing and expensive journey into the interior of Louisiana, and ultimately into Texas, for the purpose of rescuing a minister of the Cumberland Presbyterian Church, for whom he entertained a warm regard, from the suspicion which had fallen upon his Christian character in consequence of certain defamatory reports.

From the time of his removal to Natchez, troubles may be said to have begun to darken over his house. A severe shock to his constitution, caused by injuries received from the upsetting of the stage in which he was returning from the meeting of the Synod of Columbus, in the fall of 1845, impaired his health, and was the precursor of other more alarming affections in the region of the heart and brain. Soon after, a heavier calamity befell him in the death of his excellent wife. Financial embarrassment at the same time added to his burden of care. His afflictions culminated during the war, which commenced in 1861. In 1863, under the pressure of necessity, and in hope of finding repose and safety, he sold his house in Natchez, and returned to Mantua, only, however, to find his former beautiful home in a state of dilapidation, and to suffer, in repeated instances, violence and pillage from the bands of marauding soldiers who were scouring the country. In the same year he was called to lay in the grave a beloved daughter, whose devotion and strength of character made her the stay of his old age. These dark days of penury and sorrow passed slowly away. The needs and perils which pursued him gave occasion for fresh interpositions of that Providential mercy which he delighted to acknowledge. The ravens of God again brought meat and drink to the prophet in his hiding-place by the exhausted brook, and when he was permitted to come forth again from his retreat, it was evident to all who looked upon the lustre of his white locks and the subdued sweetness of his venerable face, that his sojourn in the desert had been a period of near and special communion with God.

His last appearance at an ecclesiastical assembly was at the meeting of the Presbytery, at Rodney, in the spring of 1870. On this occasion, and that of the meeting of Synod at New Orleans, the preceding fall, he felt that he was holding a valedictory with his brethren. The event corresponded with his expectation. Just on the eve of the reappearing of these respective bodies, he was removed to the Church of the first-born in heaven, sending with his dying breath an assurance of his continued love to his associates in the ministry and eldership, whose faces on earth he was to see no more.

The disease which terminated his life was a species of pneumonia, producing a paralysis of the lungs, and attended by great suffering. His mind was, until near his decease, clear and composed. He talked freely, delighted to dwell upon the loving kindness and faithfulness of God in all his dealings with him, and to bear testimony to the preciousness of those doctrines of grace in the faith of which he had lived, labored, and sufered.

His death occurred on the 11th of October, 1870, at Mantua. The funeral service was held in the Presbyterian church at Natchez on the 13th, and his body rests in the family-lot in the Natchez cemetery. His age was one month and nine days short of eighty-one years.

Dr. Chase's connection with the Presbyterian Church in the Southwest dates back almost to the origin of that church. He saw the rise of most of the organizations which now appear within its territory. He was personally acquainted with most of its pioneers and founders. His history brings him into association with Larned, Chamberlain, Bullen, Smylie, Montgomery, Rickow, Potts, Butler, Hutchison, and Bertron. As the last of two of this band, he was permitted to stretch his patriarchal hand in blessing over the host of younger laborers, whom he had seen enter into their fields. In his death, the last link between the present and the past is severed. That Dr. Chase was a Christian is tested by the undeviating rectitude and the unblemished reputation which, through an unusually long period and through a remarkable succession of vicissitudes, attended his life.

In youth and in old age, in affluence and in poverty, the principle that directed his course was the apostolic one, "To me to live is Christ." His preaching was made effective, not by any high order of intellect, but by the depth of his convictions and the intensity of his love for the souls of his fellow-men.

His labors as a consoler of the afflicted were peculiarly appreciated, and these, with those of the peacemaker between the disaffected, and the helper of the friendless and destitute, run parallel with his life.

From a world which had grown strange to him, and which, in its cruel shiftings, had left him in his going-out of it almost as naked as he was at his coming-into it, we cannot doubt he has passed into the rest of that heavenly home of which the Eden at Mantua, in its best and brightest days, was but an imperfect and treacherous type.

In conclusion, your committee recommend the adoption of the following resolutions:

1st, That this Presbytery, while bowed down with grief at the death of Dr. Chase, as a family bereft of a parent, acknowledge the signal goodness of God in sparing his valuable life so long, and in permitting him, under so varied and protracted an experience, to illustrate the beauty of Christian piety, and to verify the reality and sufficiency of Divine grace.

2d, That the eminent services of Dr. Chase, in planting and sustaining the religious and educational institutions of the Presbyterian Church in this portion of our land, entitle his name to a foremost place among those whom, as a church, we delight to honor, and ought to insure its grateful commemoration for generations to come.

3d, That the toils and sacrifices of that great cloud of witnesses, who formed the original members of this

Presbytery, to whom Dr. Chase has now been added, lay a solemn and definite obligation upon us, their successors, to foster the work they have begun, and to imitate, in building up the City of Zion, the self-denial, the zeal, and the holy simplicity of purpose, which they exhibited in laying its foundation.

4th, That our sympathies, as a Presbytery, be tendered to the family of our deceased friend and father, and that a copy of these resolutions be inclosed to them by the stated clerk.

(Signed) J. B. STRATTON,
GEO. HALL,
JOS. WEEKS, } *Committee.*

www.ingramcontent.com/pod-product-compliance
Lightning Source LLC
LaVergne TN
LVHW010246110826
845151LV00004B/1403
9781425523497